MARTI   TS

FOR BEGINNERS

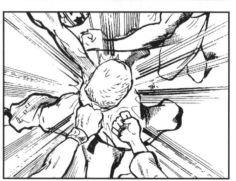

BY RON SIEH
ILLUSTRATED BY TERRY WILSON

WRITERS AND READERS PUBLISHING, INC.
P.O. Box 461, Village Station
New York, NY 10014

WRITERS AND READERS LIMITED
9 Cynthia Street
London N1 9JF
England

•

ISBN # 0-86316-171-5

0 1 2 3 4 5 6 7 8 9

Manufactured in the United States of America

Beginners Documentary Comic Books are published by Writers and Readers Publishing, Inc. Its trademark, consisting of the words "For Beginners, Writers and Readers Documentary Comic Books" and the Writers and Readers logo, is registered in the U.S. Patent and Trademark Office and in other countries.

CONTENTS

The first thing Bruce Lee said to the guy hiring him to get the bad guy in *Enter the Dragon* was **"Why doesn't someone shoot him?"** It has been said that any fool can pull a trigger and for sure, many fools have. Sometimes a highly skilled, healthy, ethical, martial artist has been the loser. Clearly the person with the gun wins so... why study martial arts?

      Good question. First, a little history.

IN THIS TOWN IT'S GUNS, SEE?

Once upon a time before the coming of firearms, the martial arts were something personal. Whether traveling outside the city gates or dwelling within, one's personal fighting art was as important as choosing a weapon is today. The coming of firearms meant that, for the first time, a person unskilled in fighting arts could defeat skilled warriors.

A strong sword arm isn't that important when all you need is a finger to pull a trigger. The arming of the American Indians changed the balance of intertribal relationships that had been relatively stable for centuries. Tactics radically changed. (Remember that old Roman wedge with their long spears and shields that was nearly unbeatable in its time? They would be sitting ducks for a group of people with long rifles.)

The various revolts of the Chinese against foreign influence during the late 19th and 20th centuries pounded home the end of non-firearm martial arts in China. The Okinawan, Japanese, Filipino, Burmese and Chinese martial arts, which at one time gave one the skills to fight and have a better chance of survival on the battle field, were almost useless.

The face of warfare had changed, delegating the non-firearm martial arts to sport or a spiritual path. Even though there is much more to survival in dangerous situations than having a gun and being a good shot when the shit hits the fan, a gun will give one a huge advantage... unless of course the enemy has guns. And then what use is a good roundhouse kick? At close range against a person with an empty or holstered gun per- haps a skilled martial artist can win, but a bullet will win the argument every time. Which brings us back to the question we started with: **WHY STUDY MARTIAL ARTS?**

I started learning martial arts quite a while ago to learn how to fight. I wasn't the bully, I was often the kid getting picked on, so having the ability to defend myself—and more importantly, having the will and the confidence to do it—was very attractive. **After a few years of serious study, confidence as well as having a skill to be proud of really started to happen, and it deeply changed how I saw myself and how I saw myself in relation to other people.**

I WASN'T AFRAID OF GETTING BEAT UP ANYMORE. CONFIDENCE AND THE ABILITY TO "TAKE CARE" OF ONE'S SELF ARE TWO GREAT REASONS TO STUDY MARTIAL ARTS.

Also the discipline and pride of achievement are very important in a young person's life. Not the kind of discipline forced on you from some resented outside authority, but *self*-discipline, making a choice to stay in the class when you are really tired and not getting retaliatory when you are hurt, stuff like that. Also having the self-discipline to end a particular training or relationship with a school and teacher when it's time.

There is a sense of initiation in the study of martial arts, something which is missing in our culture. The initiation of boys to manhood is *some*what *vaguely* part of graduating from college or high school, or joining a gang, but it is most clear in the military. For women ... what? On the other hand, there is a strong sense of accomplishment and maturity that comes with the breaking of a few boards and a new color of belt. It's formal—friends and family are there to acknowledge the ritual. You are judged by your teachers and given a handshake and the respect of older men. The schools I studied at were male dominated and the few women there often quit in a short time but my experience was years ago and times have changed. I don't know what it is like for girls learning the art being initiated into womanhood.

Along with the strength and skill that comes from the study of a martial art, comes an ability to deal with intensity. To face an "opponent" and spar or randori and do what one is supposed to do or at least try and learn from the failing can be very satisfying. In the middle of kicks, punches, throws and takedowns as well as getting hit, feeling fear and pain, is calm ... or not ... but calm is what works best and is learned in either a short or long time, depending on the student. It is relatively safe, intense with a sense of danger and fun that provide skill, health, confidence, a sense of accomplishment and an arena to watch how one's mind works! And affordable too!

IN ALL THE MARTIAL ARTS THE CRITICAL FOUN-
DATION THAT MUST BE CULTIVATED BY THE STU-
DENT IS MINDFULNESS.

Mindfulness is being in the moment whether thinking or engaged in the realm of sensation and relationship. It is pretty clear that if you are hypnotized by a good conceptual run (day dreaming), the chances are less likely of you successfully dodging

HE'S **AWAKENED** ME BETTER THAN MY **ALARM CLOCK**!

the punch or moving with the Nage or landing right after doing a flying kick. Even if we come and go between seeing pictures in our head, and seeing our "opponent," if our opponent is more awake and mindful than us, he will whack us when we are spaced.

We must make a clear distinction between **direct sensual experience,** which is relatively objective (for example, we can both look at a tree and see a tree and "objectively" it will be the same tree), and **concept** or **thinking** (for example, when we look at the tree, we can add things to the tree that "really" aren't there ...like a memory of the old

rope swing down by the river or whatever). In that case, which is **subjective**, we are not looking at the same tree. On the one hand, is the **sensation-oriented approach** (seeing, hearing, tasting, smelling); on the other hand, is **mental abstraction.** Most of the time we flicker back and forth between the two. It is to our advantage to know when we are hypnotized and when we are awake, then we can make a choice. If a stick is coming toward me at high speed I want to be in my body, awake, seeing the event as is without any mental chatter. Yes, there is intelligence without mental chatter. It is easy to confuse the mental stuff with "reality," in fact we may know someone who lives their life that way. Fundamentally confused. No problem, it is one of the central learning experiences we get ... or not ...from life.

IN MARTIAL ARTS, PARTICULARLY WHILE IN RELATIONSHIP WITH ANOTHER PERSON, "THE OPPONENT," WE WANT TO SEE WHAT IS HAPPENING WITHOUT ADDING ON STUFF THAT ISN'T THERE.

When the game gets warm it is easy to confuse potential with what the potential represents, and then we find ourselves blocking blows that aren't happening or missing the blow that does happen. Mental clarity is developed ... or not.

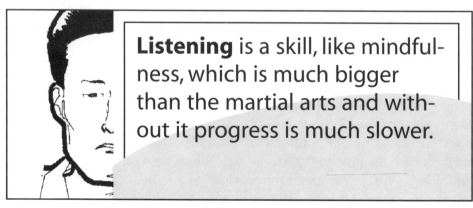

Listening is a skill, like mindfulness, which is much bigger than the martial arts and without it progress is much slower.

"Simple" listening is hearing what the teacher is saying, actually hearing it, and noticing how much we censor or opinionate or delete. Then we can do what the teacher tells us to (clearly this is in the realm of appropriateness). Listening is also the ability to "read" the "opponent"; it isn't mystical; it's simply looking and "seeing" what is there. What is open, what's not, what has to be done for the opponent to reach me, what can't be done, whether or not they are spaced out, what they are aware of and what they are not, what their parameters for openness and flow are—all that stuff and more comes from listening. Now to do that you have to be listening to yourself so you can tell your stuff from theirs. Then they can be dealt with directly, life can be dealt with directly.

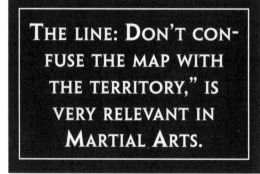

> ## THE LINE: DON'T CON-FUSE THE MAP WITH THE TERRITORY," IS VERY RELEVANT IN MARTIAL ARTS.

In this case the map is the **catalogue of techniques**, the "right and wrong" way to do things that come with any particular martial art. It is possible to do the wrong footwork and dodge the punch and do the correct footwork and get hit.

It is possible to have the correct stance that facilitates the free open movement of the Chi and not feel a thing but be totally out of the body. Depending on the teacher the student may get an endless catalogue of sets and techniques, even the "secret ninja death blow" or reeling silk or the iron palm techniques that you have to know before the other 500 preceding techniques after years of study and a lot of money. Then you get cocky, start a fight, and get trashed because all you know is techniques.

INTERNAL OR EXTERNAL; Soft or Hard

External to internal is the natural evolution of the martial artist ... or not. Over time, Karateka and Shaolin practitioners—people who study what are considered external arts—become internal martial artists ... or not.

People who study what are considered internal martial arts like Aikido or T'ai Chi Ch'uan can begin and forever remain external martial artists, thinking that the techniques and rap of the art make them internal martial artists. It's personal. It isn't necessarily the art. It is the teacher and the student; what the teacher teaches and what the student studies that will encourage or kill the movement from external to internal.

IF YOUR INTENTION IS TO LEARN AN INTERNAL ART, FIND A TEACHER WHO WALKS HIS WALK, SOMEONE WHO CAN TALK THE RAP AND HAS DEEPLY STUDIED AND CULTIVATED THE ACTUAL SKILL.

FINALLY, I'VE FOUND A MASTER WHO CAN **WALK THE WALK** OF INTERNAL MARTIAL ARTS.

LISTENING IS INTERNAL.

PLANNING IS EXTERNAL.

STRUGGLING IS EXTERNAL.

BLENDING IS INTERNAL.

BEING WITH WHAT IS HAPPENING IS INTERNAL.

WISHING THINGS WERE DIFFERENT IS EXTERNAL

BEING IN YOUR HEAD THINKING ABOUT WHAT TO DO NEXT IS EXTERNAL.

BEING IN THE BODY AND SENSATION ORIENTED IS INTERNAL.

FEELING YOUR VULNERABILITY IS INTERNAL

DENYING YOUR VULNERABILITY IS EXTERNAL

CONTRACTED, LOCKED MUSCULATURE IS EXTERNAL.

LOOSE, FLUID AND RELAXED MUSCULATURE IS INTERNAL.

Internal martial arts techniques are often more conducive to an internal approach. For example, in Aikido the Uke must blend with the Nage or they get hurt, while in Karate there is more a block - punch approach, which none the less requires correct timing (achieved through listening) to pull-off correctly.

IADO: the practice of skillfully drawing the **JAPANESE SWORD** from its scabbard. **IAIDO:** the way of the sword.

The learning of the techniques is the learning of your chosen martial art and without technique there is nothing happening. We need to learn technique, whether a side kick or swinging a stick or proper ukemi and, more: the internal is technique. Listening and blending can be considered techniques, but I think of them as the BIG techniques, the context in which all the other stuff happens. Learning to be open and mindful is paramount to *begin* to be really good at anything or that is all you can be—open and mindful—and not know any skills. So learning a martial art is learning the frills, techniques and free play peculiar to the art. Keeping in mind that that isn't "it."

A SOFT STYLE MARITAL ART IS OFTEN CONSIDERED AN INTERNAL ART WITH EXCEPTIONS LIKE HSING I CH'UAN. A HARD STYLE MARTIAL ART IS OFTEN CONSIDERED EXTERNAL WITH EXCEPTIONS LIKE ARNIS.

The best example of *soft* versus *hard* is seen in the "blocks" of the art or how a blow is avoided.

A **soft "block"** is more a parry or even a blend with the blow, redirected away from the target, or the target moved away while the "blocking" hand keeps the weapon from following the target. This is often called **checking**. A **dodge** is about the softest "block" around.

A **hard block** is just that; a hard block that stops the weapon or forces it off its trajectory. A hard block can be a **blow**. The softer the block, the less effort; the harder the block, the more power is needed. **Hard style** approaches work well when **"fighting"** a weaker opponent; **soft style** approaches work well if **you are** the weaker opponent.

KRACK!

REMEMBER, A SOFT BLOCK!

HARD BLOCKING, A LITERAL INTERPRETATION.

Harder styles tend to use raw strength to overpower an opponent, softer styles depend more on footwork and develop a more springy, whole-body power in the punches and kicks. Speed and power typify the harder styles. Speed and power also typify the softer styles, but how these are accomplished and used make the art hard or soft.

All techniques work, whether a Tae Kwon Do spinning kick, a Judo throw, a Karate punch (hard or soft, internal or external), it is also true that no technique works. Think about that! What determines the success or failure of the technique is the technique's appropriateness, the when and where of it. This includes the **timing** and **distance**, or in other words, the **relationship** between the "fighters". Without a clear sense of the rela-

tionship, it's just guess work and strategizing, and if playing with an internal martial artist, failure. Do not substitute your own intelligence and abilities for a technique or the praise of a teacher. If your particular character and stature don't fit with the teacher's objectives, shop around. On the other hand you could be a violent bully and your teacher could be trying to mellow you out a bit. A soldier of fortune or mellow out?

I MADE THE MISTAKE OF BELIEVING THAT **SAMURAIS** WERE FORMIDABLE WITH THEIR **SWORDS ONLY.** TOO MUCH T.V., I GUESS.

THAT'S ABOUT THE LAST THING I REMEMBER **NOW** I'M UP HERE **PLAYING A*HARP.** IF I'D ONLY USED MY **AK-47 BLOW-GUN** WITH THE INFRARED NIGHTSCOPE.

* the harp was made in Japan.

If you are interested in study-ing a martial art by all means shop around.

- **Talk to the teacher;**

- **talk to the students;**

- **watch some classes and notice both what is taught and how the teacher and the students relate to one another.**

If you are interested in an all knowing, God-like teacher sur-rounded by adoring devotees who think everything the teacher says is gospel, then a teacher who treats his students with respect, and where there is a mutual appreciation of each other's intelligence, won't interest you.

A MARTIAL ARTS CLASS SHOULD BE FUN.

If you don't enjoy the class but think it's more a duty, or that persevering through and suffering builds character, it's clearly time for a reality check.

GET OUT OF MY DOJO YOU WEAKLING!

Many times I have walked around places—relatively safe places—where friends of mine who are untrained in self-defense would never go alone. However, I've had friends untrained in martial arts who, if confronted with potential violence, would become dangerous. The difference is an attitude around being a victim. Sometimes training in a martial art will help change a victim-oriented attitude to one of personal responsibility. Self-confidence is a life-changing attitude, and it can be nurtured or squelched by a teacher.

OKAY LITTLE RED I'LL GO. JUST DON'T HIT ME AGAIN!

There is a trend in the martial arts to become eclectic, to combine techniques from various arts with hope of the art becoming a gestalt (or should I say *gestalted?*). (Gestalt is a German word which roughly means the whole outweighs the sum of its parts.) Too often this means learning a little bit about several arts and instead of the practitioner realizing the internal qualities that would allow appropriate action within the context of a cool technique the practitioner gathers an encyclopedia of cool techniques and no skill.

"...MOST POPULAR *OFFENSIVE TECHNIQUE* AGAINST A LEG SCISSORS ATTACK. WE ASKED *150 ADULT MARTIAL ARTISTS* FOR THE MOST COMMON ANSWER."

YIEOW!

Indeed every art has its strengths and weaknesses, different ranges of effectiveness.

For example, Karate at very close range is almost worth- less, the Karateka having to move back into a range where they can kick or hit.

KOSHI WAZA
JUDO HIP TECHNIQUE
ON KARATE-DO MAN

Jujitsu, Judo and Chin-na are the arts where grappling is studied yet at kicking range the practitioner of Judo could have a hard time. That is, until they grab the foot of the kicker. In punching range Wing Chun is a superior art.

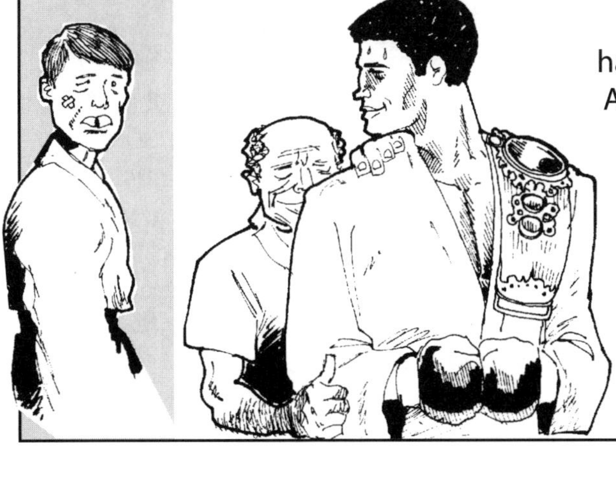

In a game of sparring its hard to beat good old American boxing. Yet again it depends on the martial artist not the art when it comes to winning or losing a fight.

This brings me to the distinction between **learning how to fight** and **learning a martial art**. They are not the same! In a martial art you learn the techniques peculiar to the art and strive to perfect these techniques. Then when you do spar with a partner you spar (sparring is not fighting) within the context of the techniques of the art. Or the techniques are replaced with something else as in the case of the earlier karate matches where no one kicked (because kicks didn't work) until a minimum number of kicks per round were made a rule. Or T'ai Chi push hands matches where the best shover wins.

HEY BLACK BELT. I FORGOT TO TELL YOU, IN STREET FIGHTING **THERE ARE NO RULES!**

YOU TELL 'IM, **BABY!**

IN A MATCH, THE RULES OF THE GAME TAKE OUT THE FIGHT AND MAKE IT SPORT.

It is closer to fighting than just practicing form after form for years thinking this will make you a good fighter but it is still not a fight. Some martial artists feel that sport matches water down the art because of the rules, and yes, I guess it does, but at least the people who do compete against another person get some real feedback concerning the effectiveness of their techniques. **Those who don't compete but only practice sets and break boards have a head full of ideas, that's when a good street fighter will beat up the black belt**.

If you want to learn a martial art for self-defense, by all means learn and get a strong foundation of a few techniques (learning five techniques and their skillful application is better than knowing fifty techniques with no skill at application).

After 65 years without a defeat, the Gracie fighting family of Brazil has now brought its victorious Jiu-Jitsu to the U.S.

*Gracie Jiu-Jitsu armlock.

Then study what it takes to do these techniques while in relationship with someone who doesn't want you to successfully do them while they try to do them to you. Study the internal principles: listening, leading, blending, flowing, etc. **This is a process of subtraction and distillation, not of addition and an accumulation of techniques.** This is what Musashi, the great swordsman of feudal Japan spoke of, and what JKD is supposed to be.

WING CHUNS
HAMMERHAND
STRIKE

WING CHUNS **HAMMERHAND** IS AT ITS BEST AS A PARRY FOLLOW-UP TECHNIQUE (1) TRANSITIONING INTO A **HAMMERHAND STRIKE** TO THE OPPONENT'S TEMPLE (2).

CHILDREN, DO NOT TRY THIS AT HOME!

If you study in an art where you compete with an opponent, you have the opportunity to explore these principles, if you don't, well, you don't. If your teacher wants you to substitute what is appropriate with proper technique, learn what is useful, then shop around for another teacher or just pretend you are too awkward to get it and study what is appropriate in class. **You can learn a lot by knowing what doesn't work.**

NOW THE **HAMMERHAND STRIKE** MAKES A FURTHER CONVERSION INTO GRAB OF THE OPPONENT'S HEAD FORCING IT INTO A **KICK (3)**.

NOT MANY MOVES IN THIS SIMPLE TECHNIQUE YET WHEN **MASTERED** IT IS QUITE EFFECTIVE. LESS WELL DONE EQUALS MORE WITH NO SKILL IN ITS APPLICATION: NEW CHINESE SAYING.

Every martial artist thinks what they do is the best. Don't get caught on this. Sure, be proud of your art, but don't do it by shitting on other arts. People who do that simply don't know what they're talking about.

Camaraderie, n o t division, should develop through compet i t i o n .

Appreciation of diversity is the Vulcan approach. Fear of difference is the product of a small mind (with potential, of course).

THAT **ESCRIMA** DEMONSTRATION WAS TRULY **OUTSTANDING!**

SO IS YOUR **STYLE**

I'LL ADD **BOTH** TO MY NIN-JUTSU.

There are three general categories of martial arts: those done for health, those where fighting techniques and application are taught, and those where one learns to fight. They interlap, of course—for example, any good workout is good for one's health (if you are physically up to it to begin with); maybe through learning some fighting techniques your natural skill as a fighter blossoms; and of course learning how to fight is extremely healthy if you successfully defend yourself against a real attack. Chi Kung and T'ai Chi Ch'uan can be not only healthy activities, but they can actually be healing and restorative. Some Aikido, while the ideal is to not hurt your attacker, often has the highest injury rate of them all. On the other hand learning how to fight doesn't involve much technique, learning techniques doesn't teach you how to fight, knowing how to fight doesn't necessarily keep you healthy.

PAUL VANUK

PAUL VANUK'S HAND-TO-HAND TRAINING OF U.S. MILITARY ALSO INCLUDE *SNICK AND SNEE SKILLS. *KNIFE FIGHTING

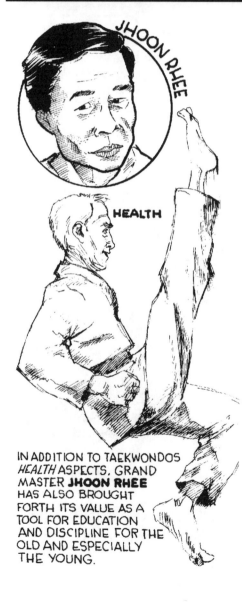

JHOON RHEE

HEALTH

IN ADDITION TO TAEKWONDOS *HEALTH* ASPECTS, GRAND MASTER **JHOON RHEE** HAS ALSO BROUGHT FORTH ITS VALUE AS A TOOL FOR EDUCATION AND DISCIPLINE FOR THE OLD AND ESPECIALLY THE YOUNG.

Wing Chun, which has techniques that are precise and efficient for fighting, is next to worthless in the hands of someone inept at sensing relationship, while **Aikido**, with its huge sweeping moves which can be relatively easily avoided and countered is, in the hands of a superior internal martial artist, an awesome fighting art.

It all depends on the teacher, what they choose to teach. People who don't teach and train the qualities that make one good at self-defense often can't do it themselves.

There are people who have internalized those qualities (listening, blending, etc.), just as there are people who have the words but nothing else, no skill.

FIGHTING TECHNIQUES AND APPLICATION

MIKE STONE

BLACK BELTS 1994 INSTRUCTOR OF THE YEAR, UNBEATEN KARATE CHAMPION AND HALL OF FAME INDUCTEE: **MIKE STONE'S** ABILITY TO TRAIN AND BUILD CONFIDENCE IS REMARKABLE.

LEARNING TO FIGHT

THE MORE EDUCATED THE PERSON LOOKING FOR A TEACHER, THE WISER THEIR CHOICE.

Sadly, most people looking for a teacher don't know anything about martial arts; that is why they are looking for a teacher. So, I'm glad you have this book.

It's a good idea to find a marital art suited to your stature. If you're big and strong, Judo or Aikido; if you're agile and quick, Escrima, Capoeira or T'ai Chi Ch'uan. Find the art that is aesthetically interesting to you. (If you are big and strong and physically suited for Judo, but the mat work of Judo bores you, you won't stay.) The world of martial arts is incredibly rich.

In the United States, we have more marital artists of different traditions than anywhere else; for some of the arts, the US has the best teachers in the world. **It's easier to find an excellent teacher of traditional Chinese martial arts in the US than in mainland China.** In China what you'll find is **Wu Shu**, Mao's "contribution" to the martial arts of China.

It is clearly not for fighting, although flamboyant and entertaining. The Wu Shu arts of Shaolin, T'ai Chi Ch'uan, Hsing I Ch'uan, Pakua Chang, etc. are not the arts of a century ago. (Even though Wu Shu teachers and practitioners often tell the naive it is the same.) Yet again, it is possible to find a Wu Shu teacher who has a firm grasp of the internal, while teachers of the traditional teach only the shapes of the art.

It is easier to find a good Escrima or Arnis teacher in the US than in the Philippines. Japan is different. People who have studied in Japan, generally find American schools a bit watered down.

CHINA

Where I will begin is China. No one really knows if it was China where martial arts in Asia started but it is romantic and mythical and it was a very, very long time ago. Besides, nearly all other Asian martial arts either have their roots in China or have been heavily influenced by Chinese arts.

There is an official origin story, which is the story of Bodhi Dharma and the temple at Shaolin. It is the standard party line and the one given to tourists. Then there is what is believed to be closer to reality.

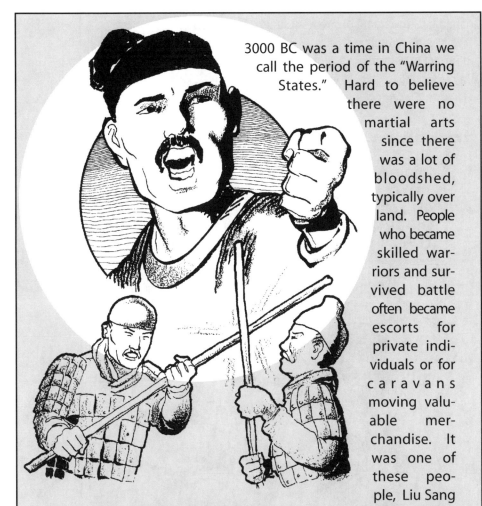

3000 BC was a time in China we call the period of the "Warring States." Hard to believe there were no martial arts since there was a lot of bloodshed, typically over land. People who became skilled warriors and survived battle often became escorts for private individuals or for caravans moving valuable merchandise. It was one of these people, Liu Sang who, while escorting a group of prisoners, freed them and led them on the rampage, "enlisting" more and more people until he had an army large enough to defeat the current ruler...and thereby became the first emperor of the Han Dynasty (202 BC to 220 AD).

SO IT'S CLEAR THAT MARTIAL ARTS WERE ALIVE AND WELL IN CHINA BEFORE THE COMING OF BODHI DHARMA—ALSO KNOWN AS TAMO TO THE SHAOLIN TEMPLE IN 540 AD.

Shaolin is the name of the temple as well as the name of the martial art that we have inherited from the first temple which is in North China (in Hunan Province) and was built around 377 AD.

Bodhi Dharma (470-543AD) was a holy man from India, a Buddhist who in the Zen tradition, formally established the Chan school of Buddhism in China, becoming the First Patriarch of that school of Zen. He is also the Patriarch of Shaolin martial arts.

Bodhi Dharma came to China around 500 AD. (give or take 30 years, depending on the source of information), and came to the Shaolin Temple on Wu Tai Mountain in the province of Hunan. There he found the monks following a sedentary life style—their routine was little more than sitting meditation—which produced sickly and weak monks.

BODHI DHARMA, UPON SEEING THEIR CONDITION, PROCEEDED TO SIT MEDITATING FOR 9 YEARS, "LISTENING TO THE ANTS SCREAM," AND WHEN FINISHED, GAVE THE GIFTS OF YIN-GIN CHING AND HSI-SWI CHING (OR TENDON CHANGING CLASSIC AND THE MARROW WASHING CLASSIC) TO THE MONKS TO INCREASE THEIR HEALTH AND STRENGTH.

Some people say that Bodhi Dharma was refused at the temple at first because of his strange teachings, then after returning years later, spoke with such authority that he demanded recognition. Fundamentally, Bhodi Dharma brought various Chi Kung to China from India.

Chi Kung is work with the breath, often with movement of some kind. Chi is energy, the electromagnetic spark of existence and Kung of course is work. There are many types of Chi, each internal organ has its own.

We humans get ours from **three main sources**—our **food** called **grain chi, air** or **breath chi**, and the **"substance"** called **Jing**, which is stored in the kidneys and is our energetic inheritance from our parents.

The first two, grain chi (chi from food) and breath chi (breath chi being trained in Chi Kung) are able to be replenished; kidney Jing is not. There are many Chi Kungs from those soft and sublime to dynamic and intense, and they are done for varying reasons, from healing, tonifying

and strengthening...to immortality—and in the martial arts tradition there are Chi Kungs that can render the practitioner impervious to blows, punches, and kicks, called "packing" or Iron Shirt Chi Kung. In fact, the boxers who revolted against the foreigners—particularly the missionaries—in 1900 (the Boxer Rebellion), were surprised when their iron shirts failed against foreign bullets.   (Or maybe that's just a good story and they were smarter than that!)

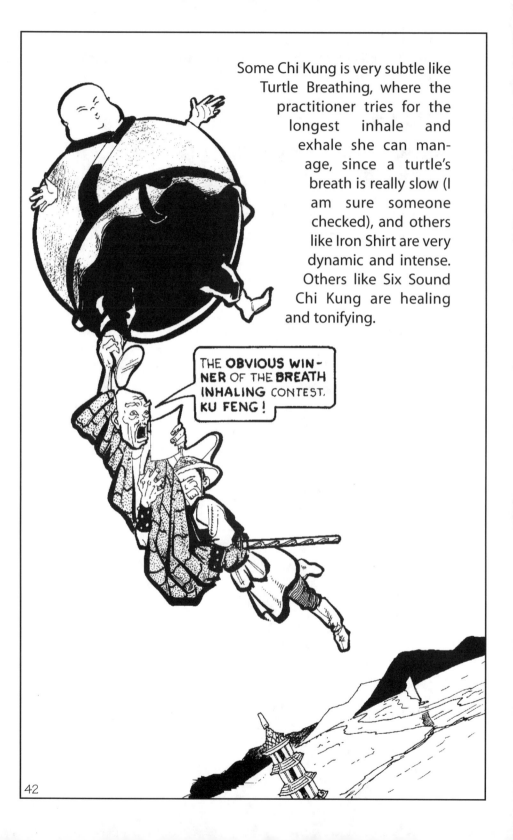

Some Chi Kung is very subtle like Turtle Breathing, where the practitioner tries for the longest inhale and exhale she can manage, since a turtle's breath is really slow (I am sure someone checked), and others like Iron Shirt are very dynamic and intense. Others like Six Sound Chi Kung are healing and tonifying.

THE **OBVIOUS WIN-NER** OF THE **BREATH INHALING** CONTEST, **KU FENG!**

THE CHI KUNG THAT BODHI DHARMA GAVE THE MONKS AT SHAOLIN, AT LEAST IN APPEARANCE, HAS LITTLE TO DO WITH MARTIAL TECHNIQUE. BY MARTIAL TECHNIQUE I MEAN THE LOOK AND ACTION OF A PARTICULAR MARTIAL ART. HOW PUNCHES ARE THROWN, HOW KICKS ARE DONE, THAT SORT OF STUFF. THERE IS ALSO THE ENERGETIC QUALITY OF HOW A TECHNIQUE IS DONE, WHETHER TENSE OR RELAXED, HOW FOCUSED, WHERE THE POWER COMES FROM, ETC. THIS IS MORE THE "SKILL" ONE GETS FROM CHI KUNG, MORE A CULTIVATION OF POWER THAN TECHNIQUE, AND POWER IS VERY IMPORTANT FOR SOMEONE WHO WANTS TO BE SKILLED AT TECHNIQUE. SO, IN THAT RESPECT, BODHI DHARMA LAID THE FUNCTIONALLY BEST AND ONLY REAL FOUNDATION OF THE MARTIAL ARTS. THE CULTIVATION OF HEALTH AND POWER.

It is clear that martial arts did not start at the Shaolin temple, the martial arts having been around hundreds of years prior, but without Shaolin and the arts created there the Asian fighting arts would be very different. The temple was a networking center for martial artists from all over. In fact, of the Chinese martial arts we see today, almost all have their roots in Shaolin.

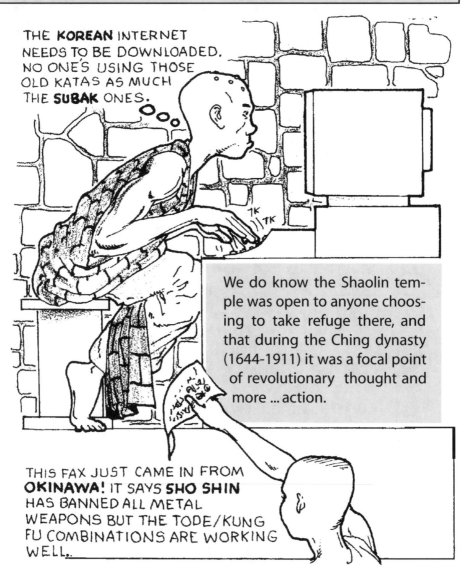

THE **KOREAN** INTERNET NEEDS TO BE DOWNLOADED. NO ONE'S USING THOSE OLD KATAS AS MUCH THE **SUBAK** ONES.

We do know the Shaolin temple was open to anyone choosing to take refuge there, and that during the Ching dynasty (1644-1911) it was a focal point of revolutionary thought and more ... action.

THIS FAX JUST CAME IN FROM **OKINAWA!** IT SAYS **SHO SHIN** HAS BANNED ALL METAL WEAPONS BUT THE TODE/KUNG FU COMBINATIONS ARE WORKING WELL.

The hot radical enthusiasm of the Shaolin bred more than one martial art that they thought would help them defeat the Manchus. During the Ching dynasty, the Manchu were the ruling class and were often allied with the British against those rebellious Chinese peasants. When the Shaolin temple was burned in 1768 by the Manchus, the martial artists fled and taught their arts all over China. One place several fled was to Fu Kien province in southern China where another temple was built (we think) and then burned by the Manchus.

It is encyclo-pedic in depth and scope. There are usually **ten** sets (depen-ding on the school), that are learned and they are flashy and dynamic and, as I have said, encyclopedic, containing the extensive repertoire of Shaolin techniques. The stances are typically long, as are the punches, with high to low kicks, sweeps, grappling or Chinna flips and trips. This is the time to introduce the term **Kung Fu** (or *Gung-Fu* in Cantonese). Kung Fu means **"skill achieved over time through practice."** For a skilled plumber, plumbing is his Kung Fu, for a skilled musician it is music. Even for a beginner there is a field of study that is his Kung Fu. His Kung Fu is very high or very strong or very young or very poor.

One's Kung Fu is his discipline. The phrase Kung Fu is bigger than just martial arts, yet

since we are talking about martial arts, when I use the phrase Kung Fu you will know what I'm talking about. **What I'm talking about is Chinese martial arts.** The Kung Fu Bodhi Dharma introduced to the monks at the temple was his Chi Kung, a discipline of breathwork and movement for healing and strengthening. What sprouted from this was Northern "Sil lum", (in Cantonese transliteration) or Northern Shaolin.

47

800 years after the arrival of Bodhi Dharma, a monk named Chueh Yuan perfected what he thought was an incomplete system of martial arts at the temple. He developed a 170 move system which he then divided into five subdivisions. **These are the five animals of Shaolin:**

- The **Crane** system, which strengthens the sinews.
- The **Leopard**, which develops speed and power.
- The **Tiger**, which develops strong bones.
- The **Snake**, which strikes vital points.
- The **Dragon**, which builds a strong spirit.

Each of these styles has a particular stance, footwork, favored weapons and specific techniques that are peculiar to the system. Tigers claw and rip, cranes poke and evade, and snakes are poisonous. Each system has a trademark fist, a crane's beak, a leopard fist, or a tiger's claw for example. The five together are called **Shaolin Kung Fu.**

Shaolin is the granddaddy martial art and the techniques of its subdivision arts which were mostly developed in the 18th and 19th centuries are all found in Shaolin. Most fighting arts in Asia, whether Japanese, Thai, or Filipino have been influenced by or have their roots in Shaolin. The marital arts that follow have each focused on a particular range and style, and each is a piece of Shaolin.

THE ARTS ARE OFTEN PRACTICED SOLO IN WHAT ARE COMMONLY REFERRED TO AS SETS (OR KATA IN JAPANESE OR OKINAWAN, AND HYUNG IN KOREAN). THESE ARE CHOREOGRAPHED STRINGS OF MOVEMENT WHICH ARE THE PARTICULAR TECHNIQUES OF THE ART.

FOUR CHINESE BROTHERS PRACTICING **JAMES WING WOO** SINGLE HAND TAI CHI.

SCISSOR AND OPENING   WT. SHIFT   PRESS   PUSH   49

Periodically, throughout history, martial arts were banned in many countries by rulers who felt threatened; since the arts were banned, their practice went underground, often preserved through dance and sets. Sets are also done solo and the practitioner would not have to risk injury to himself or opponents to practice his art. There are also two-person sets, still relatively safe, yet closer to combat. In Chinese, Japanese, Okinawan, and Korean martial arts the practice and study of solo sets is the foundation of the art.

NOT **ANOTHER ONE** OF THESE **KICKING DANCES** CANT THESE **SLAVES** DO ANYTHING **ELSE**? LIKE A **TANGO** OR **SKA JERK**?

THE MA STANCE (OR HORSE STANCE) IS CHARACTERISTICALLY SHAOLIN AND IS FOUND IN ALL FORMS OF KARATE. KARATE IS OKINAWAN OR JAPANESE.)

Usually it was practiced along with punches for quite a while to strengthen the legs before further techniques were taught. Often

weights or stone blocks would be held in the hands while the practitioner threw punches to strengthen the stance and arms.

Body strengthening exercises such as pounding and slapping the limbs and torso are done to enable the student to take

blows. The rubbing of shins and forearms against the edge of a table (or something similar) for hardening the limbs is common; it is often followed by the application of Dit Pat Jow, a bone medicine used to prevent bruising.

There is a training called Iron Palm (which is done several ways depending on the lineage) where the hands are toughened, often by slapping a bag filled with Iron shavings or Iron BBs then the application of medicine to prevent deforming the hand. There are stories of people who could pierce rhinoceros hide with their fingers but couldn't pick up a coin because of lost sensitivity and deformity of the fingers.

51

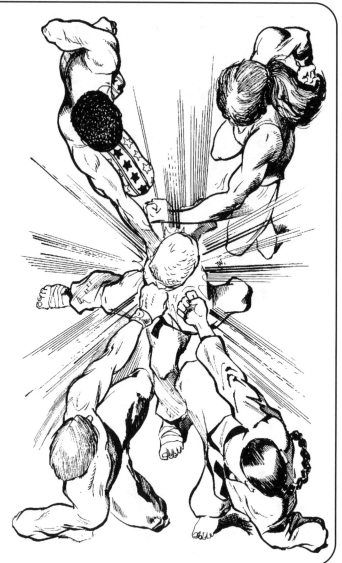

Depending on the teacher, many or no Iron techniques are taught. Iron shirt, for example, which "toughens" the whole body against blows, is common to most arts yet seldom taught and it can vary in training from school to school.

NORTHERN OR SOUTHERN?

It is a common belief that the Chinese martial arts that are considered Northern are a bit more dynamic, using longer stances, deep punches and high flashy kicks, while Southern styles—those developed at the Southern temple—are more short-punch, and low-kick oriented, short power being a focus of study in the south.

NORTHERN STYLE
LOOKS VERY GOOD
ON TELEVISION.

Wing Chun is considered a Southern style martial art because of its popularity in Hong Kong, rather than its place of creation. It has an origin story which gives the flavor of Shaolin politics. In the early 18th century when the Hans were ruled by the Manchus, the Shaolin temple was a place where, among other things, people were trained to be martial artists who would fight against the Manchus. Five Grand Masters got together to develop a martial art that could be mastered in less than a decade rather than the two decades the mastery of Sil lum would take. Unfortunately, before this new art was developed, the temple was burned by the Manchus. One of the Grand Masters escaped. What is interesting is that this master was a nun. Her name was Ng Mui and she taught an orphan girl by the name of Wing Chun. Why did the only surviving Grand Master of Shaolin teach an orphan girl and only an orphan girl? I don't know. Wing Chun then taught her husband Lenng Bok Cho, thus creating the patriarchy of Wing Chun masters that continues today.

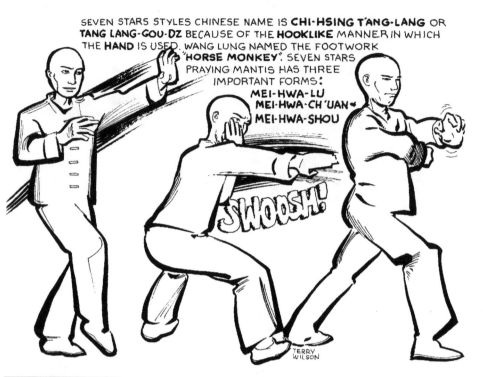

SEVEN STARS STYLES CHINESE NAME IS **CHI-HSING T'ANG-LANG** OR **TANG LANG-GOU-DZ** BECAUSE OF THE **HOOKLIKE** MANNER IN WHICH THE **HAND** IS USED. WANG LUNG NAMED THE FOOTWORK "**HORSE MONKEY**". SEVEN STARS PRAYING MANTIS HAS THREE IMPORTANT FORMS:

MEI-HWA-LU
MEI-HWA-CH'UAN
MEI-HWA-SHOU

SWOOSH!

TERRY WILSON

Praying Mantis

Praying Mantis Kung Fu was created by a Shaolin disciple named **Wang Lang** around 1700. He watched a praying mantis fight a cicada, (some say a grasshopper), and saw in the fierce (fierce for a bug), scissors-like actions of the praying mantis, the making of a martial art. **He combined the praying mantis hand techniques with the stepping of a monkey and created his Kung Fu.** It's called **seven stars** style after the constellation Pliades. More like a Southern style, the kicks are low with a lot of hand techniques, grabbing, tearing and gouging as well as punching. There is also **six harmonies** praying mantis, a style founded by Wei San—the harmony being between the eyes, hand, body, spirit, chi, and mind—and **eight steps**. Eight steps was created by Chun Hua Lung, who was influenced by some Hsing I and Tom Bei (two other martial arts) friends. He wanted to create footwork to get in closer and Hsing I footwork fits the bill.

54

Monkey

Monkey style, created by one Kao Tze in the 1800s, is one of the most entertaining and strange styles. Kao Tze, a man already trained in martial arts, observed and classified the movements of monkeys. The practitioner really tries to take on not only the movement of a monkey, but its spirit, acting shy and timid to fierce and aggressive, with kicks, sweeps, punches, gauging, etc.

ON MY RIGHT DECEPTIVE **WOOD MONKEY**. THIS IS GOOD "EXTERNAL ANIMAL FLAVOR".

BUT "INTERNAL ANIMAL FLAVOR" IS MORE DESIREABLE.

MONKEY **GROIN ATTACK** OF **TALL MONKEY**

THE 5 MONKEY CATEGORIES
LOST MONKEY
DRUNKEN MONKEY
TALL MONKEY
STONE MONKEY
WOOD MONKEY

KAO TZE DEVELOPED THE MONKEY KUNG FU WHILE IN PRISON FOR EIGHT YEARS,

"**MONKEY STEAL THE HEART**"

BY WATCHING THE **MOVEMENTS** AND **BEHAVIOR** OF **MONKEYS HE SAW** FROM HIS CELL WINDOW.

55

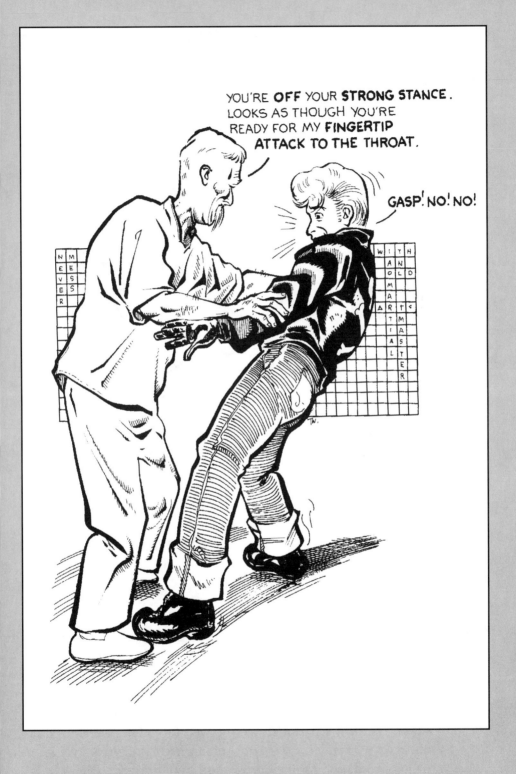

There is even a drunken monkey, hard to hit, elusive, staggering around as if drunk—until it mounts a hidden attack! Cleverness and deceit are qualities of monkey style. There are five monkey styles: **drunken, stone, lost, standing, and wooden**

Eagle Claw

Eagle Claw, created by the Chinese general Oak Fay in the 12th century, used a lot of **joint locks, ripping and gouging** (as you would guess from the name). It is similar to Chinna, which is the art of grappling. Eagle Claw practitioners learn 108 striking points which are acupuncture

points and can sting, immobilize, cripple, or kill whoever is hit hard enough. It's similar to Ju-Jitsu (a Japanese art) in its subduing and controlling (rather than punching) techniques. It is not as flashy and hard to learn as Sil lum, but clearly the techniques are dangerous.

Southern Styles

Choy Li Fut, which is very common in Hong Kong, was created by Chan Heung in 1836. He combined the Kung Fu of the Choy and Li families and the Kung Fu of a Buddhist monk named Cheng Chao Her Shang, a teacher of Shaolin Choy Fook. After getting good at Shaolin, he created Choy Li Fut. Fut refers to Buddhism in Chinese, so he honored his Shaolin teacher. Chan Heung was one of the martial artists who actively taught the Manchus, training people in Choy Li Fut. Choy Li Fut contains five standard animal forms similar to Shaolin: **snake, crane, tiger, dragon**, and **leopard**.

USUALLY CHO LI FUT CONTENDERS HAVE TO DEVELOPE EXPERT **LONG HAND SKILLS**.

Hung Gar

Hung Gar is the Kung Fu style of the second Shaolin temple in Fu Kien province. Created by the Hung family (Gar means family), some scholars say it is Northern Shaolin without the high kicks and acrobatics, simply *called* Hung Gar to disguise it and keep it from the Manchus. The monk Chi-Sim apparently made his way to Southern China after the burning, but the true origins are ambiguous. Hung was a student of Chi-Sim.

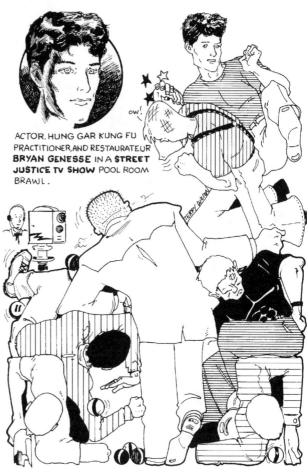

ACTOR, HUNG GAR KUNG FU PRACTITIONER, AND RESTAURATEUR **BRYAN GENESSE** IN A **STREET JUSTICE TV SHOW** POOL ROOM BRAWL.

White Crane

White Crane (also known as Tibetan White Crane since it was originally created in Western China) became popular in Southern China. Like the internal art of T'ai Chi Ch'uan, the practitioner never uses force against force but uses the opponent's strength against him. It uses long punches, with no grappling (Chinna) and evasive circular (Pakua-like) foot-work and high kicks. A trademark of the system is the hand called a Crane Beak, in which all the fingers are straight, the wrist is bent, and those fingers meet each other in a crane-shaped point.

CHON TO DESTROY   SIM TO EVADE   CHUN TO PENETRATE   Jeet TO INTERCEPT

The philosophy of White Crane

SING-LUNG IS CREDITED WITH INTRODUCING **WHITE CRANE** TO CHINA. A STYLE COMPOSED OF 24 SETS: 10 EMPTY HANDS AND 14 WEAPONRY.

A. **WILLOW LEAF KNIFE**

B. **SPEAR** WITH TASSEL TO ENTRAP WEAPONS OR CONFUSE OPPONENTS

C. **BUTTER FLY KNIFE**

JICK BOWLOK LOWLOW, OR **NG·MUI** IN CHINESE, IS CREDITED WITH DEVISING THE **"MU-FA-JEONG** *PLUMFLOWER STUMPS.

Wing Chun

Wing Chun is one of the most well known of Southern Kung Fu, no doubt because it was the art that the late **Bruce Lee** first learned. Wing Chun is efficient, compact, and relatively simple, with few techniques compared to other styles. Wing Chun has only three forms. Again, it is an art with origins at the Northern Shaolin temple.

> THE NORTHERNERS CREATED WHAT THEY CALLED WING CHUN, WHICH MEANS "HOPE FOR THE FUTURE."

Apparently the Manchu employed "traitor" monks to fight against the rebellious Shaolin. Wing Chun was a new direction for the temple against the Manchus. Alas, the temple was burned before the new art was taught and the nun Ng Hui who was one of the creators of the new style, escaped to a nunnery on Tai Lenng mountain.

61

There she taught an orphan girl whom Ng Hui named Wing Chun. Wing Chun taught her husband Lenng Bok Cho,x creating the patriarchal lineage of Wing Chun masters. It is considered a Southern martial art because of where it was made public—in Hong Kong in 1952 by Yip Man.

Some people say there are two styles of Wing Chun. One watered down and simplified and less mobile, the other with opportunities to step and move. Other people say this is untrue. **Chi Sao** is the **Wing Chun two-person practice** where sensitivity is trained and is similar to two-person exercise in T'ai Chi Ch'uan call **Tui Shou**.

It is a simpler system, with less content than other Chinese martial arts, only having three solo sets, plus some **wooden dummy** work, and, of course, **Chi Sao.**

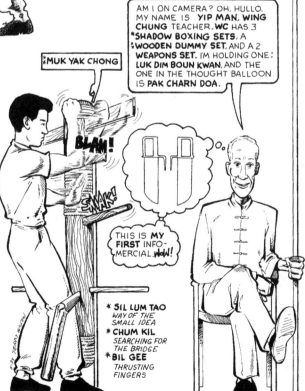

In all the Shaolin arts, a strong, healthy body is a priority since it is hard to fight if you are sick. Simple to exotic body-conditioning exercises are common to all the schools and styles. Stretching. strengthening, and hardening drills are done to many different degrees, depending on the teacher.

Usually these are the arts that people, preferably as children, will start with since the stretching and strengthening is important simply to get, and stay, strong and limber. And the flashier and more dynamic nature of the sets simply looks cooler and is more fun than the "internal" martial arts.

THIS WORKED "*THE 36th CHAMBER*" KUNG FU MOVIE, BUT **BETTER WAYS** OF STRENGTHENING THE BODY ARE **NOW USED**.

WATCH THAT SLOSHING **BUCKET** SAN TE!

FRONT BENDING

LEG STREECH

When Americans think of Kung Fu, it is usually one of these arts, and there are many more styles of this art than are described here. When the martial artist is concerned with power, particularly more relaxed and effortless power, her art turns internal no matter the style. But there are martial arts that start where training in the Shaolin arts lead. They don't look as flashy but the fireworks are inside. These martial arts are called Nei Chia, or internal school martial arts.

63

EXTERNAL AND INTERNAL

There are two traditions of Chinese martial arts and they are the so-called **external** (or outer) and **internal** schools or **Wai Chia** and **Nei Chia**. These two schools are also called **Shaolin** and **Wu Dang**. It is said that the *external* martial arts, which Shaolin is said to be, are mainly concerned with *strengthening the muscles and bones and achieving the proper execution of technique*, while *internal* arts are more concerned with the *cultivation of Chin (intrinsic power) and the more "energetic" skills of listening to and reading an opponents movement and presence.*

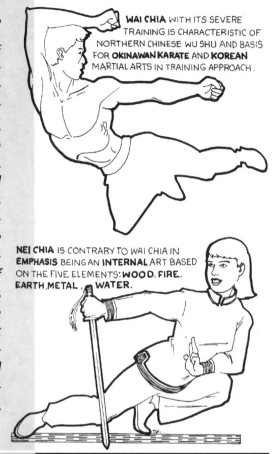

WAI CHIA WITH ITS SEVERE TRAINING IS CHARACTERISTIC OF NORTHERN CHINESE WU SHU AND BASIS FOR **OKINAWAN KARATE** AND **KOREAN** MARTIAL ARTS IN TRAINING APPROACH.

NEI CHIA IS CONTRARY TO WAI CHIA IN **EMPHASIS** BEING AN **INTERNAL** ART BASED ON THE FIVE ELEMENTS: **WOOD, FIRE, EARTH, METAL, WATER.**

THE EXTERNAL IS HARD, OFTEN CALLED A HARD STYLE. KARATE IS OFTEN CONSIDERED A "HARD" STYLE, HARDER AND FASTER BEING TWO OFTEN USED WORDS BY INSTRUCTORS TO STUDENTS.

THE INTERNAL IS SOFT AND RELAXED, MORE CIRCULAR, TIMING BEING MORE IMPORTANT THAN SPEED, WHILE BODY MECHANICS AND OPENNESS TO THE OPPONENTS INTENT ARE MORE IMPORTANT THAN THE EXECUTION OF A SPECIFIC TECHNIQUE.

For example when faced with a punch from a right hand coming toward your face an external or hard stylist would see this as a challenge and a problem to be thwarted and overcome, usually by **blocking** the punch and trying to **hit** or **kick** the puncher. An internal martial artist could avoid the punch through **listening** and **dodge** the punch **without interfering with it**, perhaps even use the puncher's own force to "help" him off balance and throw him. In Aikido, a Japanese internal art, the attacker would (ideally), not be harmed. This was important to Ueshiba the founder (if not some of his followers). There would be a quality of openness to the event that the hard stylist would not have.

ASIDE FROM HARD BLOCK **EXTERNALS** AND CIRCULAR EVASIVE **INTERNAL** STYLES ARE THE EXHIBITIONIST HARD STYLE OF ICE BLOCK SHATTERING AND CHI FORCE REPELLING OF AN OPPONENT.

GRUMP!

65

Instead of trying to interfere with the punch and direct the event to their advantage through force, the event would be seen, listened to, adhered to, blended with, and concluded. An internal martial artist feels the situation and fills the holes. Or not.

Actually, there are not any entirely internal or external martial arts (Shaolin and Wu Dang more accurately describe the categories), but there are internal or external martial artists. The hard styles of Shaolin or Karate can be done as delicately and naturally as a soft or internal style.

That is when the internal "style" is demonstrated by internal artists. I've seen a lot of Aikido and T'ai Chi Ch'uan which are considered

"HOW I MISREAD **KATHY LONG** AND LOST!"

KATHY LONG, LOVELY AND TOUGH **KICKBOXING CHAMPION**, IS ALSO AN ACTRESS AND **DOUBLED** FOR **MICHELLE PFEIFFER** IN **BATMAN RETURNS** AND CLOBBERED THIS **OTHER FIGHTER**.

UNG! I WAS **SO BUSY** WATCHING FOR HER KICKS, I **FORGOT** TO LOOK OUT FOR HER **TNT** FIST!@!※!!

internal styles done in a contrived and stubborn style. External to internal is a natural progression of skill rather than any particular art. My Tae Kwon Do teacher (Tae Kwon Do is a

Korean art) was, when I studied with him, an internal martial artist while his art, Tae Kwon Do, is typically considered hard and external.

Any situation or relationship— including one of potential violence— demands a certain openness, a "feel" for the lover's or enemy's or friend's intentions. To "feel" an opponent's intention requires feeling our own vulnerability—and that is an asset rather than something to deny. Denial is denial: to rather not feel something in ourselves is to deny the situation as it is, to misread it.

Misreading is the number one reason people "lose" fights, or miss the Frisbee, lose at Chess, miss the ball, trip, injure themselves, get in fights, etc. etc.

Something that all Chinese martial arts have in common is the notion of cultivation and storing energy in the Tan Tien (in Chinese) or Hara (Japanese). This is a point in the human body two or three fingers' width below the navel and perhaps one-half to one and one-half inches inside the abdomen, depending on the tradition ... or, more importantly, where the person *feels* it is. It is where the breath is concentrated in many Chi Kungs and where one's vitality is stored. Chi or energy is also central to Chinese martial arts. In fact, it is central to all martial arts, though, more often than not, it is spoken of more or less after the basic techniques of the art are learned. The internal branch of martial arts is called Wu Dang after a range of mountains in Hubei province. T'ai Chi Ch'uan (T'ai Chi Ch'uan means Supreme Ultimate Absolute, Ch'uan is boxing), the most popular of Wu Dang arts, was created by Chang Seng Feng according to the legend ascribed to by the Yang family. Chang Seng Feng, apparently already skilled in Shaolin (and a Taoist), retreated to the Wu Dang mountains in 1327 and there witnessed a battle between a snake and a crane.

(In fact the witnessing of animals fighting is found in the origin stories of several martial arts.) Anyway, Chang Seng Feng was impressed with how the snake did not fight the strength of the crane or did it block the crane's blows -- it avoided them. Chang Seng Feng thereupon realized the advantages of yielding to force rather than fighting it, which is a central theme in T'ai Chi Ch'uan. Chang Seng Feng's birthday is said to be on April 9th and is celebrated by T'ai Chi players worldwide.

THE INTERNAL ARTS ARE CONSIDERED TO BE A BLEND OF TAOIST ENERGETICS AND BREATHWORK, AS WELL AS THE TAOIST APPROACH TO THE WORLD AND MARTIAL TECHNIQUE.

Philosophically, one cannot speak of Chinese internal martial arts without speaking of Taoism. The Tao (pronounced "Dow"), is the equivalent of the Dharma in Buddhism, God in Judaism and Christianity, or "What Is" or "Suchness" in Zen.

Lao Tzu

The most famous and well read work on Taoism is the "Tao Te Ching" or "The Way and the Power." According to legend, it was written by Lao Tzu around 500 BC (Lao Tzu means old teacher), but no one really knows if he wrote it or if the "Tao Te Ching" was written by several authors over a period of time. The legend says that Lao Tzu, being fed up with the folly of his fellow humans and their chasing after worldly gain, decided to give it up and head for the hills.

At the city gate he found the guard would not let him do so unless he **wrote down** his wisdom, thus the "Tao Te Ching."

Lao Tzu, unlike Confucius, disdained social convention and also ... religion. **The experience of Tao does not come from faith or acting the way we think we should, but from the depth of our own nature.** There is a quality in Lao Tzu's Taoism of "beginner's mind," of raw, naked experience, unencumbered by philosophy or rules. Chapter 18 is one of my favorites:

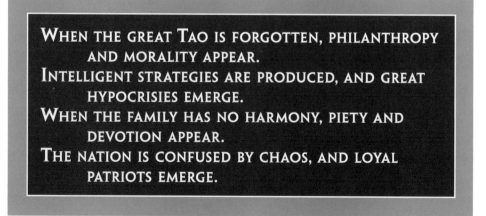

> WHEN THE GREAT TAO IS FORGOTTEN, PHILANTHROPY AND MORALITY APPEAR.
> INTELLIGENT STRATEGIES ARE PRODUCED, AND GREAT HYPOCRISIES EMERGE.
> WHEN THE FAMILY HAS NO HARMONY, PIETY AND DEVOTION APPEAR.
> THE NATION IS CONFUSED BY CHAOS, AND LOYAL PATRIOTS EMERGE.

Taoist martial artists or internal martial artists approach the experience of combat with this quality of spontaneity and lack of contrivance.

There are different approaches to Taoism. Confucius was really into virtue, familial piety and

one's place in the structure of society. I like to say that Confucius would have one obey and faithfully fulfill one's societal and familial obligations to realize Tao, and the Lao Tzu "approach" is to naturally realize the Tao through deep yet

simple opening to the Tao. One is a process of duty and addition, the other a process of openness and subtraction— subtracting the layers of socialization, contrived duty, and obligation. You can see which of the two the Chinese government ascribes to, and which, in turn, can be used to justify a

bureaucratic government. The other approach—the openness and spontaneity of Lao Tzu and Chuan Tzu Taoism—is called Wu Wei.

Wu Wei, or "non-action," is not doing nothing, but doing nothing in excess.

Excess can mean eating when you are not hungry, sleeping when you are not tired, defending yourself when you don't have to, being afraid of something that doesn't exist, blocking a punch that isn't there, wanting to be different than you are, thinking too much, being tense, worrying, making excessively long sentences and the list goes on.

REALIZING ONE'S OWN NATURE IS THE HEART OF TAO.

INTERNAL ARTS

The arts described so far are all considered Wai Dan or external school. Nei Dan or Nei Chia, which means internal school, are the arts originating from Chan Sang Feng. Wu Dang is where Chang Sang Feng created his T'ai Chi Ch'uan, the external are Shaolin. The internal arts are T'ai Chi Ch'uan, Hsing I Ch'uan, and Pakua Chang and have been influenced by Taoist thought, Chi Kung, and healing work and are generally done in a more relaxed (but not excessively relaxed) manner.

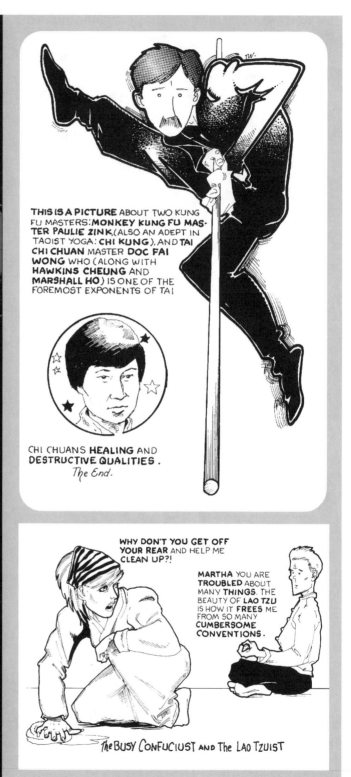

THIS IS A PICTURE ABOUT TWO KUNG FU MASTERS: **MONKEY KUNG FU MASTER PAULIE ZINK**, (ALSO AN ADEPT IN TAOIST YOGA: **CHI KUNG**), AND **TAI CHI CHUAN** MASTER **DOC FAI WONG** WHO (ALONG WITH **HAWKINS CHEUNG** AND **MARSHALL HO**) IS ONE OF THE FOREMOST EXPONENTS OF TAI

CHI CHUANS **HEALING** AND **DESTRUCTIVE QUALITIES**. The End.

WHY DON'T YOU GET OFF YOUR **REAR** AND HELP ME CLEAN UP?!

MARTHA YOU ARE **TROUBLED** ABOUT MANY **THINGS**. THE BEAUTY OF **LAO TZU** IS HOW IT **FREES** ME FROM SO MANY **CUMBERSOME** CONVENTIONS.

THE BUSY CONFUCIUST AND THE LAO TZUIST

T'AI CHI

T'ai Chi Ch'uan is the most popular of the internal arts. T'ai Chi means **supreme undifferentiated ultimate absolute**; Ch'uan means **fist**. A tall name for a martial art to live up to. After Chang Sang-Feng, the history of T'ai Chi Ch'uan is ambiguous until Chen Wang Ting in 1618. The existence of Chang Sang-Feng is disputed by some historians who insist it was created by the family of Chen-Chia Kou during the Ming dynasty. Others say it was taught to the Chens who had their own brand of Kung Fu by Wung Tsung-Yeuh. He beat up the Chens who challenged him as he was traveling through Chen-Chia Kou, so they asked him to stay and teach. Whatever the origin, Chen style is considered the **original T'ai Chi** and the other styles of T'ai Chi Ch'uan come from it. There is an older style systematized by Chen Chang-Hsin and a newer style which is a bit simpler without the flashy kicks created by Chen Yu-Ben.

Chen style is the **flashiest** of T'ai Chi styles, using a whip-like motion for power and some fast explosive punches and kicks. It, like most T'ai Chi, is done in slow motion except for a few quick movements. Breathing is usually attended to as well, exhaling when extending (such as punching or kicking), inhaling when contracting. Depending on the school, **normal breathing** (in which the belly expands when inhaling and contracts when exhaling), or **reverse breathing** (the stomach contracts on the inhale and expands on the exhale) is taught.

The first is typically called **Buddhist** breathing; the latter, **Taoist** breathing. In Chen style can be seen its Shaolin origins, at times looking like slow motion Shaolin. In appearance, it is the most martial of the T'ai Chi Ch'uan styles.

YANG STYLE HISTORY

Yang style, created around 1820 by Yang Lu Chan, is the most popular of T'ai Chi Ch'uan styles. According to the Yang family T'ai Chi players

who ascribe to the Chang Sang-Feng origin story of T'ai Chi, Yang became employed by the Chens as a servant when he expressed his interest in learning their T'ai Chi and was refused. Yang was already skilled at Shaolin and stayed on to learn the Chen family art.

SO ONE DAY HE HEARD THE SOUNDS OF TRAINING AND PEERING THROUGH THE FENCE WITNESSED THE CHENS PRACTICING THEIR ART.

He memorized what he saw and practiced in private. He was eventually found out and when asked to show what he knew, the Chen's were so impressed by his skill they accepted him as a student. He then took T'ai Chi Ch'uan outside the Chen village and taught throughout northern China. (I don't know how the Chens felt about this.)

He even went to Beijing to teach the royal family, although some T'ai Chi players think what he taught them was a watered down version—after all the royalty were the hated Ming—and taught the real stuff to his sons Pan-Hou, (1837-1892), and Chien-Hou, (1835-1917). Some say the watered down version is too soft with no Peng or ward-off energy which empowers the set. This is the art as popularized by Yang Chen Fu. There is ongoing controversy concerning what is good T'ai Chi Ch'uan and what isn't; all you can do is study with someone who has the skill to match his claims.

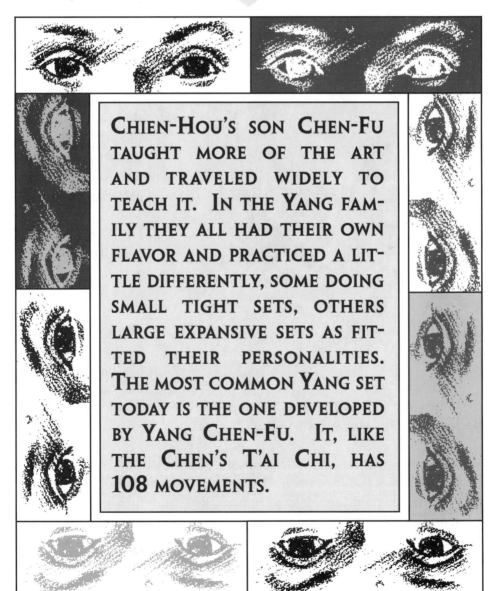

CHIEN-HOU'S SON CHEN-FU TAUGHT MORE OF THE ART AND TRAVELED WIDELY TO TEACH IT. IN THE YANG FAMILY THEY ALL HAD THEIR OWN FLAVOR AND PRACTICED A LITTLE DIFFERENTLY, SOME DOING SMALL TIGHT SETS, OTHERS LARGE EXPANSIVE SETS AS FITTED THEIR PERSONALITIES. THE MOST COMMON YANG SET TODAY IS THE ONE DEVELOPED BY YANG CHEN-FU. IT, LIKE THE CHEN'S T'AI CHI, HAS 108 MOVEMENTS.

CHENG MAN CHING

DR. CHENG MAN CHING 1902-1975
POET, CALLIGRAPHER, PAINTER, **CHENG** BEGAN **TAI CHI** WHEN HE WAS 25 FOR **HEALTH**; IT RESTORED IT. **TAI CHI** AS A **HEALING ART** HAS A LONG HISTORY IN **CHINA** ADDING TO ITS REPUTATION AS A **COMBAT** ART. **CHENG** WAS **TAI CHI'S** GRANDMASTER.

TERRY WILSON

Northern Tai Chi Ch'uan (or, more specifically, Tai Chi Ch'uan in the United States), while currently represented by three main styles (Chen, Wu, and Yang) and variations in emphasis, which range from New Age fluff to slow motion Shaolin (and from external to internal) — and everyt h i n g i n between — cannot be spoken of without mentioning Chen Man Ching.

Cheng Man Ching studied with Yang Cheng Fu, and although he most probably studied with others during his life (he died in 1973), he declared he only studied with Yang Cheng Fu.

There are several Yang style Tai Chi sets. The most popular long set is Yang Cheng Fu's 108 move set. Cheng Man Ching took out some repetitive moves, like two sets of Wave Hands Like Clouds and one set of Step back and Repulse Monkey and many Brush Knee Twist steps, etc., plus moves he considered "double weighted" (a move where the lead foot and the "head" hand are on the same side—like a jab) like Fan Thru Back and developed a shortened set of around 18 moves (depending on how it's counted). The Short Set is the most popular set in the U.S., many teachers adopting it, some changing its flavor and design.

Cheng Man Ching style is more than a set of movements; it is softer with a shorter stance that is shoulder width and roll back energy or yielding is its hallmark. Cheng Man Ching was supreme at the two person practice Tyi Shou or push hands, yet because of his softness and stance and insistence on yielding, it is not Yang style. It is Cheng Man Ching style. Yang style—at least Yang Cheng Fu's and Pan-Hou's style—has a longer and narrower stance, but more importantly, the hallmark of Yang (and Chen) style is not roll back energy or yielding, but Peng or ward-off-energy.

Some people say the softer style was taught to these nasty Manchu royalty by the Yangs, and it was not the martial Tai Chi done for power but Tai Chi done for health and relaxation. Others say when Cheng Man Ching fought or used push hands, he clearly used ward off energy artfully combined with the softer yielding, but he didn't teach it. Hard to say why.

In Tai Chi Ch'uan, one school's relaxed is another school's stiff. What good Tai Chi Ch'uan is depends on the intention, skill, and functional ability of each individual. Very relaxed and loose can work or not, depending on the individual. It is very important to find a teacher who can demonstrate what he or she is talking about.

77

WU STYLE

Wu Yu-Hsing (1812-1880) studied with Yang Lu Chan and Chen-Chin Ping, started his own school of T'ai Chi, which he called appropriately **Wu Style.** His style was closer to the original Chen style than to modern Yang style.

T'AI CHI CLASSICS

Although the three styles look different, the underlying principles are the same. Several books collectively known as the "T'ai Chi Classics" outline the principles of T'ai Chi Ch'uan. They are: *T'ai Chi Ch'uan Ching*, attributed to Chang Sang-Feng; *T'ai Chi Ch'uan Luu*, by Wang Tsung-yueh; *Expositions of Insights into the Thirteen Chapters*, by Wu-Yu-hsiang; *Five Character Secret and Essentials of Form Practice and Push Hands*, by Li-I-Yu, who was student of Wu-Yu-Hsing's; and *The Song of 13 Postures*, and *Song of Pushing Hands*, by unknown authors.

Whatever the school, the words relax, sink, and unify are often used to describe the practice. Depending on the school, how these are accomplished differs. *Relax*, to some schools, means *unified* to another; *sink*, which means low stances to one school, can mean feeling grounded to another.

All schools practice Tui Shou or pushing hands, which is a fluid two-person exercise that is the foundation of T'ai Chi for self-defense. Tui Shou uses four of the original postures—**Ward Off, Roll Back, Press, and Push**—and can be practiced with stepping or fixed step. There are pushing hands competitions through out the United States and although relaxed power (Chin) and yielding and re-directing the opponents strength is the ideal, the competition can quickly degenerate into a bullying and shoving match.

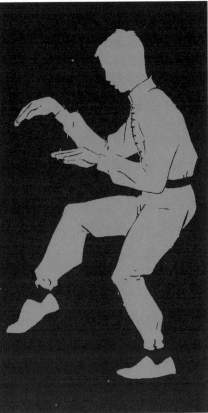

Then, depending on the school, Ta Lu is taught, then San-Shou. Ta Lu uses four more of the 13 postures of T'ai Chi Ch'uan: **Elbow stroke, Shoulder stroke, Pull down, and Split**. The other five of the 13 postures are: **Advance, Retreat, Gaze to the Right, Look Left, and Central Equilibrium**. These last five are not confined to any single technique; they represent the quality of all-inclusive attention.

The moves of the T'ai Chi set correspond to the trigrams of the *I Ching* or *Book of Changes*. In fact, eight of the original thirteen postures are represented in the Pakua Emblem.

THE FIVE THAT ARE LEFT CAN CORRESPOND TO THE FIVE ELEMENTS OF CHINESE MEDICAL THEORY.

YIN AND YANG

Yin and Yang are two movements of the formed universe—one contracting, the other expanding; one cold or hot, male or female, day or night. Although nothing is solely Yin or Yang, everything has either a Yin or Yang expression. In T'ai Chi, a forceful move such as a punch or push is Yang, while yielding is Yin. A foot that is weighted is Yang, while the unweighted is Yin. One yields to the opponent's Yang and fills in what is Yin. Yin and Yang are complementary parts of the whole and harmonious in nature. In Chinese medicine a balance natural to health is desired while an imbalance causes disease.

T'ai Chi philosophy can get very complicated and scholarly and often doesn't have that much to do with real skill in the art, one being experiential and the other conceptual ... and after all, T'ai Chi Ch'uan is a Taoist art.

SOLO AND TWO-PERSON WORK

San Shou can either be a long, choreographed, two-person set using all the moves of the solo set, or open, free sparring, or free play. The study of the principles are the real practice of T'ai Chi Ch'uan. Listening, leading, sticking, neutralizing, and discharging are the central skills of T'ai Chi for self-defense. The cultivation of Chin or intrinsic strength is cultivated in the solo set, and the other skills can only be learned in the two-person practices. Relaxation, sinking, and unification or integration are the foundation without which there is neither root or power. Depending on the teacher, the art is either an exercise for health or a martial art which also produces health and much more. It is fundamentally a practice of awareness... or merely a choreographed set of movement. It depends on the teacher.

T'AI CHI CH'UAN IS MEDITATION IN MOVEMENT AND MANY PRACTICE FOR THIS QUALITY OF THE ART ALONE. IT IS ALSO A HEALING CHI KUNG WHICH, UNLIKE HARDER STYLES OR AEROBIC EXERCISE (LIKE RUNNING), DOESN'T PUT STRESS ON THE JOINTS AND IS EASY ON THE BODY AND MIND.

THIS MAY RESEMBLE A **FRED ASTAIRE** DANCE SEQUENCE, BUT ITS A **JIANSHU** SWORDPLAY KATA.

Although the practice of the solo sets without the two-person work can be meditative and healing, it lacks the substantial quality that the self-defense aspects give the art. In relationship with another person, we get feedback concerning the principles of **relax, sink, and unify.** If the practitioner does not yield to a push, she gets unbalanced or "uprooted." If he doesn't dodge a punch or neutralize a shoulder stroke, he gets hit or bumped by a shoulder. In the two-person work,

> IN THE TWO-PERSON WORK, THE T'AI CHI PLAYER WANTS TO BLEND WITH AND LEAD THE ACTIONS OF THEIR PARTNER AND... ALLOW THEIR PARTNER TO DEFEAT HIMSELF.

the T'ai Chi player wants to blend with and lead the actions of their partner and in that non-interfering, Taoist way, allow their partner to defeat himself.

The skills of listening, blending, and leading are usually not explored without the two-person practices. Yet here again the sets, whether two-person or solo, can be done in a spirit of open exploration or robot-like adherence to how the practitioner thinks it should be done. One way is internal, the other external.

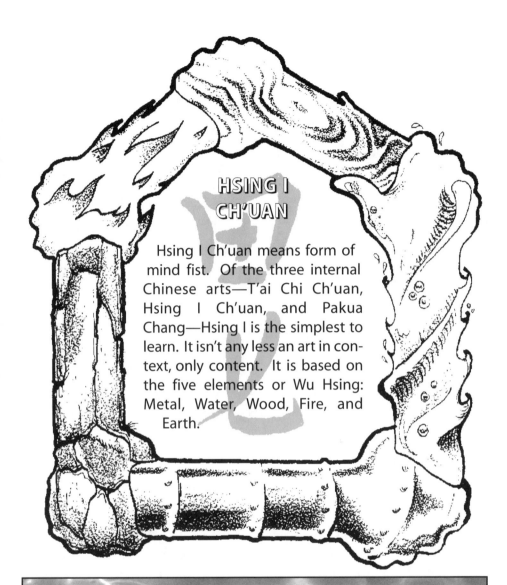

HSING I CH'UAN

Hsing I Ch'uan means form of mind fist. Of the three internal Chinese arts—T'ai Chi Ch'uan, Hsing I Ch'uan, and Pakua Chang—Hsing I is the simplest to learn. It isn't any less an art in context, only content. It is based on the five elements or Wu Hsing: Metal, Water, Wood, Fire, and Earth.

THE ELEMENTS CORRESPOND TO FIVE ACTIONS OR BLOWS WHICH ARE:

Rising, Falling or Splitting	P'i Ch'uan	Metal	Lungs
Drilling	T'suan Ch'uan	Water	Kidneys
Shooting like an Arrow or Crushing	Peng Ch'uan	Wood	Liver
Cannon Firing or Exploding	Pao Ch'uan	Fire	Heart
Crossing	Heng Ch'uan	Earth	Spleen

THERE IS A CREATION CYCLE OF THE FIVE ELEMENTS AND A DESTRUCTIVE OR MODIFYING CYCLE.

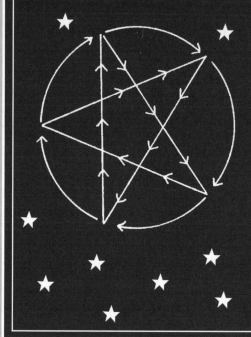

Metal creates **water** creates **wood** creates **fire** creates **earth**. It is easy to see how they fit together except for metal creating water. Well, water will form on metal in the form of condensation as the temperature changes, right? The elements in Chinese medicine are more functions and qualities than real elements ... and each of the five fists in Hsing I have different appearances as well.

The modifying cycle goes: **metal** modifies **wood** modifies **earth** modifies **water** modifies **fire**. In Chinese medical theory, without organs modifying or having a leash on other organs, the organs would overheat or over-tax other organs while not nourishing others. The five fists in Hsing I are said to balance and strengthen the internal organs (like T'ai Chi and Pakua) and are first studied solo, then in two-person practice called **San Hat.**

Several joining sets which combine the elements are learned along with stepping patterns which are important in all martial arts.

Then there are the **twelve** Hsing I animals, each with their own mini-set:

swallow, **falcon**. **eagle**, **bear**, **turtle**, **dove**, **dragon**, **snake**, **horse**, **tiger**, **monkey**, **rooster**.
(There are actually three styles of Hsing I, and each one has a different set of 12 animals.)

Again, these are first learned solo, then studied in two-person practice called On Tsan Pau.

SOME HISTORIANS BELIEVE THAT HSING I WAS CREATED AT WU DANG MOUNTAIN LIKE T'AI CHI; SOME SAY IT WAS CREATED AT SHAOLIN. AGAIN, IT IS HARD TO KNOW ITS TRUE ORIGIN.

Its origin and creation is generally credited to **Marshal Yeuh Fei** during the northern Song dynasty (960-1129). During that time he joined the Song army to help northern China fight off a raiding nomadic people from the north. He proved himself in combat and soon became a general, instituting the learning of martial arts in the basic training.

The martial art he created and taught his troops was Hsing I Ch'uan. Yeuh Fei is also credited with creating a famous external Chi Kung called "Eight Pieces of Brocade."

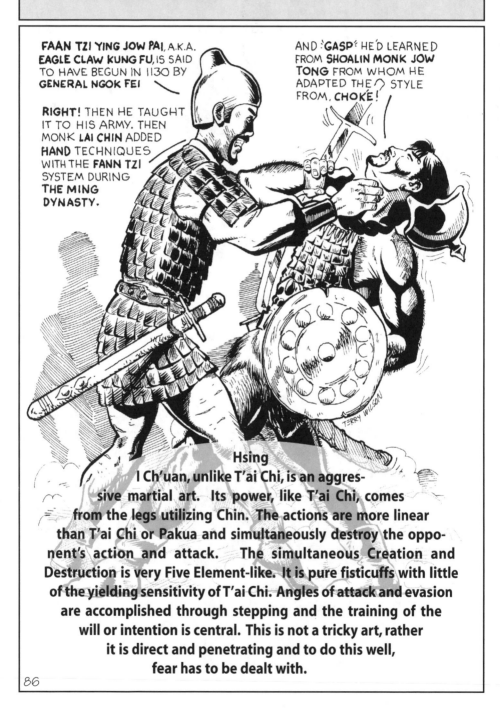

FAAN TZI YING JOW PAI, A.K.A. EAGLE CLAW KUNG FU, IS SAID TO HAVE BEGUN IN 1130 BY GENERAL NGOK FEI

RIGHT! THEN HE TAUGHT IT TO HIS ARMY. THEN MONK **LAI CHIN** ADDED **HAND** TECHNIQUES WITH THE **FANN TZI** SYSTEM DURING THE MING DYNASTY.

AND 'GASP' HE'D LEARNED FROM **SHOALIN MONK JOW TONG** FROM WHOM HE ADAPTED THE ∩ STYLE FROM, **CHOKE**!

Hsing I Ch'uan, unlike T'ai Chi, is an aggressive martial art. Its power, like T'ai Chi, comes from the legs utilizing Chin. The actions are more linear than T'ai Chi or Pakua and simultaneously destroy the opponent's action and attack. The simultaneous Creation and Destruction is very Five Element-like. It is pure fisticuffs with little of the yielding sensitivity of T'ai Chi. Angles of attack and evasion are accomplished through stepping and the training of the will or intention is central. This is not a tricky art, rather it is direct and penetrating and to do this well, fear has to be dealt with.

PAKUA

Pakua Chang means **Eight Trigrams Palm**. Pakua Chang functionally is based on the circle. Seeing the solo set being done, it's hard to see how it is used as a martial art. There are no punches and very few kicks. It is more Chinna (joint locking) oriented than fisticuffs. In fact some people, typically Pakua people, say that when the founder of Aikido, Morehei Ueshiba, traveled in China, he encountered Pakua, thus inspiring him to modify his Aiki Jutsu.

The first thing the Pakua practitioner learns is to **"walk the circle,"** placing one foot ahead of the other like walking a tight rope. Where Hsing I Ch'uan uses a more vertical power, Pakua uses **horizontal power,** sweeping and locking the opponent. The movement of the hands are called **Changes** and how many the practitioner learns depends on the school.

In Pakua **stepping** is key, the practitioner spinning and quickly reversing the spin around her opponent, slapping away punches and hitting with the palm, or elbow.

LIKE T'AI CHI CH'UAN AND HSING I CH'UAN, THE CULTIVATION OF CHIN IS CRUCIAL, YET IN PAKUA THERE IS A COILING AND RELEASING ACTION, WHICH, WHEN PERFECTED, IS THE SOURCE OF PAKUA POWER.

The origin of Pakua Ch'uan, like most Chinese martial arts is vague and ambiguous, yet there is a generally believed origin story, sometimes with a real person at the beginning. For Pakua, the real guy at the (maybe) beginning was **Tung Hai-Chuan**. Pakua is the newest of the Chinese traditional arts and was (or wasn't) created by Tung **around 1850**. Tung was apparently skilled at other martial arts and some say he learned something close to Pakua from a Taoist hermit. Again, it is hard to say what the truth is. There are several different styles of Tung's Pakua, since it was modified by his students **Yin Fu** and **Cheng Ting-Hua**.

ITS PHILOSOPHICAL BASE IS THE I CHING, THE BOOK OF DIVINATION. IT IS CONSIDERED THE MOST ESOTERIC AND HARD TO LEARN OF THE THREE INTERNAL ARTS. HSING I IS THE SIMPLEST, THEN T'AI CHI.

The one Chinese (from China) teacher (called Sifu, pronounced see-foo) I have had who was willing to talk about his training said it was slow.

For example, one of the weapons of his system (which was southern praying mantis) were the butterfly knives (not to be confused with the balisong, the Filipino flip knife). He said that before they would teach him any knife sets, he would throw a potato in the air and cut it in two ... many times ... with many potatoes. Then his teachers would show him something and wouldn't show him any more until he got very good at what they did show him.

His teachers would not do a lot of explanation of technique—they would leave its "meaning" open to discovery. The lack of explanation would (ideally) prevent the student from "locking" the technique into one application or use. This guy said that explanations were what the modern Chinese are good at ... and Americans.

This teacher is old school, a rare breed. Who is to say what teaching style is better? (I prefer open-ended explanations.)

Often there is no ranking system in Chinese styles—or if there is, it is something new to the style, something for Americans. In the ranked systems I have had personal experience with, a belt often means length of time practicing rather than level of skill.

Although a person's skill usually improves over time in the schools (I studied Karate-Do, and Tae Kwon Do), at the school where I studied, there were green belts who were more skilled than some black belts and brown belts who could beat up black belts and of course there were the killer black belts no lower belt could touch but were the people who could beat up most of the school's black belts when they were only purple belts.

BRUCE LEE AND JEET KUNE DO

Jeet Kune Do means "The Way of the Intercepting Fist." First, it was not Bruce Lee's wish to create a style, something that someone could look at and say, "Oh, that's Jeet Kune Do." Jeet Kune Do is a concept, a way of being in a fight. What Bruce Lee tried to do was to bring intelligence into what he saw as dogmatic and crystallized Chinese martial arts.

Typically, what the student of any martial art will be told by his instructor is that there is a right and a wrong way to do a technique—and I agree there is—but it has little to do with the mimicking of the way someone else does it. How it feels, is it powerful, are more important. Adaptability and flow?—if something doesn't work, flow in to something else; your opponent dictates the proper technique. Bruce Lee trained what he called attributes; timing, distance, flow, and natural ability as much as a particular technique.

This sounds like the typical internal marital arts rap, and it is, yet the difference between the words and reality are light years apart. It is rare to find someone authorized to teach Jeet Kune Do (JKD). Dan Inosanto, Richard Bustillo, Larry Hartsell, Paul Vunak are, and not many more than that.

ONE OF THE TWO ORIGINAL SURVIVING JEET KUNE DO INSTRUCTORS, **MR. INOSANTO** ALSO TEACHES **ARNIS DE MANO, KALI, SILAT, KUNTAO**, AND MORE! HE'S FOUNDER OF THE ONLY **PHILIPPINE MARTIAL ARTS ACADEMY** IN SOUTHERN CALIFORNIA. A KEY DEVELOPER OF JUN FAN KICKBOXING, HE'S AUTHORED BOOKS AND APPEARED IN FILMS. MEET **DAN INoSANTO**

ANOTHER ONE OF THE TRUE TEACHERS OF **JKD** CONCEPTS AND **FILIPINO KALI ACADEMY** BOARD MEMBER IN TORRANCE, CA., **MR. BUSTILLO** ALSO CHAIRS ON THE JEET KUNE DO SOCIETY. HE'S BEEN INSTRUMENTAL IN PRESERVING AND HONORING BRUCE LEES MEMORY. **RiCHARD BUSTILLO**

PAUL VUNAK

CERTIFIED BY **DAN INoSANTO** IN **JEET KUNE DO CONCEPTS** AND **FILIPINO MARTIAL ARTS. MR. VANUK** HAS BLACK BELTS IN TAE KWON DO AND KEMPO KARATE, TEACHES SAVATE, AND HEADS **PROGRESSIVE FIGHTING SYSTEMS**. THE **NAVY SPECIAL FORCES UNITS** HAVE RECEIVED INTENSE TRAINING FROM HIM. A MAJOR TEACHER AND <u>PROMOTER</u> JKD CONCEPTS.

Ironically JKD people have been criticized for teaching drills and technique and little more. JKD is individual, personal, and spontaneous—more a journey into self-expression than the learning of techniques.

A **FORMLESS FORM**, SHAPELESS, LIKE **WATER**. NOW YOU PUT WATER INTO A CUP, IT **BECOMES THE CUP**. SOFT TO THE TOUCH, YET ABLE TO BEAR GREAT SHIPS. HOW CAN **I FIND A WAY** TO **EMPTY MY** MIND AND **BECOME LIKE WATER**?

Bruce Lee's foundation, his first and only formal training in the martial arts, was with the Wing Chun Master Yip Man in Hong Kong. (One must have a foundation.)

Then he moved to Seattle, then taught awhile the San Francisco Bay area. While in the Bay area something happened. (Whatever did happen, it was not what happened in the fictional movie  about Bruce Lee's life, *Dragon*.) Bruce Lee realized the limitation of adhering to any style and opened his relationship to martial arts to create Jeet Kune Do. The style that is not a style.

Although Lee called his art a way (Do), yet, unlike Karate-Do and Judo, it is a fighting art where anything goes and it is trained that way, with gloves, mouthpieces, and lots of training equip- ment. I don't think Bruce Lee brought anything new to the world of martial arts historically, but he did bring something fresh and powerful to the modern world of martial arts.

OKINAWA

Okinawa is the birthplace of modern **Karate**. Originally the Okinawans called their art simply "Te," meaning *hand*, or Bushino-Te, which means warrior's hands; it was practiced before what the Okinawans call Chinese Kempo arrived in the 14th century. Kara, which was originally used in Okinawa, is an ideogram that means or refers to China thus, **Kara: Chinese. Te:hands**. Gichin Funakoshi changed this ideogram to mean **empty hands** in the 1930s.

In 1392, a group of Chinese settled in Okinawa for purposes of trade negotiations; they also taught Chinese Kempo or Kung Fu. Some Okinawans went directly to China to learn martial arts and to bring their skill back to Okinawa.

IN 1470, WEAPONS WERE BANNED IN OKINAWA AND AS A CONSEQUENCE THE WEAPON-LESS FIGHTING ARTS FLOUR-ISHED.

(The techniques of Te were also hidden in the Okinawan folk dances for preservation and to escape detection from the monarch Sho Hashi in the 15th century and later in the 17th century by the Japanese.)

An art called Kobudo was practiced by the commoners; what was special about it was the use of common tools as weapons, like the ton-fa—the wooden handle that was inserted in a hole in the side of the millstone they ground grain with—or the nunchaka (remember Bruce Lee in the film *Enter the Dragon*), which was a flail to separate grain from the chaff.

There are several schools of Karate in Okinawa and they have all taken on some Japanese influence to varying degrees. The Japanese approach is more linear in the **blocking** techniques and there is a tendency towards a "harder" style. What the Okinawans call Chinese Kempo was pretty much what was practiced before the Meiji Restoration in 1868, after which Okinawa really started to feel Japanese pressure to modernize.

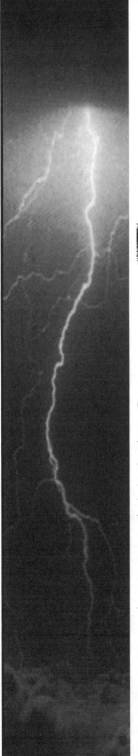

In 1922, Gichin Funakoshi, an Okinawan Karate Sensei (Sensei is the Japanese word for teacher), was invited to Japan to demonstrate his techniques. His art was well received and he taught at several Universities in Tokyo. Funakoshi's art is called Shotokan and Shotokan Karate; it is the most popular Karate outside of Japan and Okinawa.

The style that is more closely akin to the earlier Kempo style, and is more popular in Okinawa, is called the Goju style or Goju Ryu. Ryu signifies a Rynkunu martial art, Okinawa being part of the Ryuku Islands.

This style was founded by Shogyun Miyagi who became the Karate hotshot in Okinawa after Funakoshi left for Japan.

It seems odd that Shotokan is the harder style since Gichin Funakoshi was a little guy while Miyagi was big and strong. Usually one wants to find a martial art that suits his or her stature and it is typical that people create martial arts that emphasize what they are good at. All karate is thought to be harder, emphasizing hard blocks rather than softer parries or dodging and is more linear than the softer, rounder, Chinese martial arts. This is a generalization but it is typically the case.

AMONG OTHER HONORS, MIYAGI'S WORK WITH THE **OKINAWAN** POLICE HAS BEEN MEMORIALIZED BY A **BRONZE BUST** OF MIYAGI AT ONE OKINAWAN P.D.

All those kick katas! Overcoming samurai we Okinawans have a fraction of the kicks Chinese and Japanese use. I'll be well rested for my next encounter.

TERRY
WILSON

All the techniques in Karate are found in the Chinese arts, the big difference is what is emphasized and the training methods. While there are front kicks, back kicks, side kicks, round kicks, spinning kicks, tornado kicks, crescent kicks, hooking kicks, and more types of kicks in Shaolin, there are only a few of those (like the front, back side and round kicks) used in Okinawan Karate.

THE TRAINING, DEPENDING ON THE TEACHER, CAN BE INTENSE, REALLY EMPHASIZING PHYSICAL STRENGTH AND ENDURANCE. THE PLACE WHERE THEY TRAIN IS CALLED DOJO AND DOJO ETIQUETTE, AS IN THE JAPANESE ARTS, IS VERY IMPORTANT.

Karate has a ranking system, starting of course at white belt working one's way through a group of colors, often yellow, green, purple or blue, red or brown, then black, sometimes with stripes— meaning what degree of a particular belt, like second degree brown for example. The colored rank before black is called Kyu, and black and beyond Dan, a second degree black belt being second Dan. The Dan rankings are Shodan, Kodan, Sandan, Yodan, Godan, Rodudan, Shichidan, Hachidan, Kudan, and Judan.

In America, a black belt is usually the end goal after a few years of training. In Okinawa and Japan, a black belt means the fundamentals have been realized and the time for deeper training is to begin.

A few American Martial Arts Notables

1. **BILL** "SUPERFOOT" **WALLACE** 2. **JOE LEWIS** 3. **ED PARKER**: FATHER OF AMERICAN KEMPO 4. **CHUCK NORRIS** 5. **JOE CORLEY** 6. **STEVE SANDERS**: CO-FOUNDER OF BLACK KARATE FEDERATION 7. **EMILIO BRUNO**: JUDO PIONEER AND INSTRUCTOR **8 ANTHONY MARAKIAN**: KARATE PIONEER AND INSTRUCTOR. HERE ARE JUST A FEW AMERICAN MARTIAL ARTS TRAIL-BLAZERS WHOSE DEVOTION, SELFLESSNESS, SKILL AND INTEGRITY HAVE BLESSED MARTIAL ARTS NOT JUST IN AMERICA, BUT **WORLD OVER**!

Gichin Funakoshi is the father of Japanese Karate, more that than a representative of the Okinawan Karate that he learned from the Masters of Okinawan Te, Azato, Itosu, and Matsumura. He simplified the Okinawan art, so, as he said in his *book Karate-do, My Way of Life*, "...to be simple enough to be practices without undue difficulty by everybody." Whew! I can see how some would glean from this that he either popularized in Japan a watered down art for simply that, popularization, or ... revenge for the Meiji Restoration. Just kidding!

His changing the character Kara from Chinese (hands) to Empty (hands) was very controversial and upset both Okinawans and Japanese (even though Kara as Empty is as fundamentally appropriate as the character meaning Chinese—probably more so since Karate is not a Chinese martial art even though its roots are in China—and Empty refers to a Zen term, "The Void," and Japanese arts are greatly influenced by Zen). He also suggested the art be renamed to Dai Nippon Kempo Karate-do, or Great Japan Fist Method Empty Hands Way. Great Japan Fist Method? Hmmmm....

He was also against the naming of his art Shoto-Kan, which it is called today. Shoto was Funakoshi's pen name and Kan is house, so Shoto-Kan, the house of Shoto.

When Funakoshi learned the art, it was illegal. The people who learned it had to really show a teacher (an illegally teaching teacher) their desire to learn, often dramatically, not just having the money to pay the tuition. Although Funakoshi had some great students, most were college students ... or the ruling class, diletante-ing around.

101

THE WAY

Before we go on, I should talk about Do, or "The Way." Karate-Do is Funakoshi's art; prior to that, either just Te or Bushinote, warrior's hands, sometimes Karate Jutsu. Jutsu is a fighting art, in fact, it is a warrior's art, the battlefield art -- including everything a warrior should know to survive the battlefield.

TADASHI YAMASHITA

Archery, swordman-
ship, horsemanship,
various weapons, an
empty-handed fight-
ing system (well
rounded, from grap-
pling to fisticuffs),
survival and first-aid.
A "Do" is an art, hav-
ing more spiritual,
perfection-of-self
overtones. (When I
perfect my side kick, I
perfect my spirit—
that sort of stuff.)
Great stuff, but I think
the guy with the per-
fect side kick would
have been one of the
first to go on the bat-
tlefield. "Do" has cre-
ated an environment
in which the martial
arts are studied as a
reflection of oneself,
where one hopes to
transcend or trans-
form oneself into
one's ideal. This is
very important in our
modern times and
self-discipline is what
is trained in Do.

103

I have heard a rumor that after the Japanese defeat of W.W.II, when martial arts were outlawed in Japan by the Allies, several Jutsu were changed to Do, thereby passing themselves off as spiritual arts rather than fighting arts.

Typically a Do is a spiritual oriented, some would say watered down, version of what was originally a fighting, thus, killing art. This is a discussion in itself since most artists in the "traditional" arts do spar but pull punches in training. Like Karate Do practitioners (yes, they say they are traditional) saying that they practice a killing art, never having killed or been in a real fight, or even sparred with full contact with mouth-pieces and gloves.

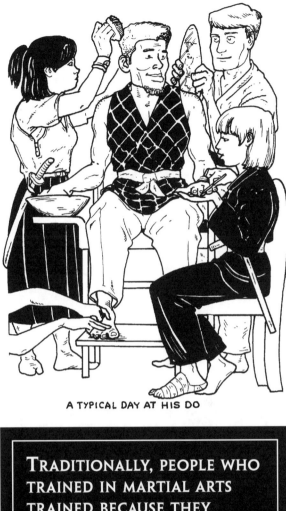

A TYPICAL DAY AT HIS DO

> **TRADITIONALLY, PEOPLE WHO TRAINED IN MARTIAL ARTS TRAINED BECAUSE THEY FOUGHT AND HURT OTHER PEOPLE. THE MODERN MARTIAL ARTIST SELDOM IF EVER DOES.**

In fact the only "proving ground" or barometer for their skill as fighters is sparring. True sparring is not fighting, but it's a lot closer to it than simply punching the air and saying to yourself, "If I hit someone they would die."

First off it can be pretty hard to hit someone who doesn't want to get hit and most don't. Also it is hard to hit someone with power since distance and angles are always changing and most martial artists simply cannot hit hard while moving. In the sport of non-contact sparring, it is called point karate, where points are tallied for supposed hits rather than, say, a knock out. I trained in Tae Kwon Do this way, and when I was pressed to use my art, I found out in no time that, having trained for years how *not* to hit someone, I was ... good at it. I could also break a lot of wood. As the great one, Bruce Lee said in *Enter the Dragon*, "Boards don't hit back."

Another reflex punching drill with **Mr. 12" x 12"**, the insolent **piece of wood**!

WHEN **DROPPED** THE **TANG SOO DO** MAN HAS

TO...HE **HAS TO HIT MR.12"x 12"** IN MID-AIR TO IMPROVE HIS **PUNCHING REFLEXES.**

EVENTUALLY, **HE DOES !**

TRAINING, DISCIPLINE, AND AN OPPORTUNITY TO BREAK THROUGH PHYSICAL AND EMOTIONAL BARRIERS AS WELL AS THE CULTIVATION OF COMRADERIE ARE OFFERED BY THE DO ARTS.

Kumite is the Japanese word for sparring, and one style in particular—in fact, the most popular in Japan—does a lot of it, with little if any protective gear. It was created by the prodigious **Masutatsu Oyama.**

So, on the one hand we have "traditional" Karate that preserves and prac-tices the art in Kata or choreographed forms of techniques, sparring without making contact, and breaking a lot of stuff. On the other hand, we have contact sport Karate, where practitioners still do Kata but have modified the art to be better able to win in the ring.

Many of the contact fighters have trained in Western style boxing because the bobbing, weaving, punching, and the training of mobility often wins in the ring against more "traditional" Karate players or Karateka. Traditional-ists dog sport Karateka for diluting the art and continuing a fighting art to sport rules. Sport Karateka dog traditionalists for being unrealistic and out of touch

MAS OYAMA HAS AN ANNUAL KNOCKOUT TOURNAMENT

IN OKINAWA THE MAIN STYLES OF RYU ARE:

Shito Ryu, which is a blend of Goju Ryu (which is a softer style) and Shorin Ryu, a harder style. It was created by Kenwa Mabugi, who also studied with Kanryo Higaonna, as did Chojan Miyagi the founder of Goju Ryu.

Goju Ryu, which is softer, more circular, closer to Chinese Kempo than Shito Ryu. Created by Chojun Miyagi.

Shorei Ryu, which is a style closest to the original Okinawan art of Naha-Te.

These are only three out of the many, many Ryu practiced in Okinawa.

JAPAN

Japanese Karate is typically a bit more linear with harder blocks and a plowing through the adversary attitude. There are softer styles of Karate such a s Wado Ryu but generally they are pretty hard.

Gichin Funakoshi, who I have already mentioned, was the first to make a powerful impact in Japan with his art of Okinawan Karate. His pen name Shoto was used by his students (apparently he didn't like it) in describing the art, Shoto-Kan, the Hall of Shoto. Today in America it is the most popular of Japanese Karate. When someone says they study Karate-Do it is typically Shoto-Kan.

THE STANCES ARE LONGER AND THE PUNCHES DEEPER THAN SOME OTHER STYLES; THEY ARE TRADEMARKS OF SHOTO-KAN.

In Karate, "traditional" Karate (what "traditional" is, is questionable), which Shoto-Kan is (sort of), the punches are fired from the hip, starting with a fist with the fingers up cork-screwing towards the inside until the fist is flat with the fingers down at the finish of the punch.

The theory is this will suck the opponent into the punch. In Chinese Kung Fu the fist is usually a standing or vertical fist because the horizontal fist is a bit easier to catch in an elbow lock.

GRANDMASTER **KANRYO HIGA** (SHI) **ONNA** 1851-1915 ANAHA-TE MASTER, OKINAWAN KARATE PIONEER, AND CONFUCIAN SCHOLAR. HE SPENT AT LEAST TWENTY YEARS IN CHINA STUDYING CHINESE KEMPO UNDER **LIU LIU KO.** AFTERWARDS HE INTEGRATED **GO-NO** (SOFT) KEMPO AND **JU-NO** (HARD) INTO ONE SYSTEM. "THOSE WHO LEARN KARATE SHOULD HELP OTHERS..."

KENWA MABUNI 1889-1957. OF **SAMURAI LINEAGE**, HE BEGAN STRENUOUS KARATE TRAINING AT 13, INCLUDING WEAPONS. **YASUTSUNE ITOSU** ALSO INFLUENCED HIS CREATING OF **SHITO-RYU.**

CHOJUN MIYAGI 1888-1953 FROM SEPT. 1902 TO OCT 1915 **KANRYO** TAUGHT HIM **NAHA-TE.** HE STUDIED **CHUGOKU** KEMPO IN CHINA FROM NOV.1915-17. UPON RETURN TO OKINAWA HE INSTRUCTED ITS POLICE. CHOJUN WAS ONE OF KARATES BEST ORGANIZERS AND PROMOTERS, AND TEACHERS.

THE SANCHIN STANCE: GOJU-RYUS TRADEMARK

3 GOJU-RYU KATAS

TERRY WILSON

There are Karate styles popular in Japan that are closer to the Okinawan "original" popularized by Okinawans who arrived in Japan after Funakoshi.

—**Goju Ryu**, popularized by Miyagi Choijun who studied under Higaonna. Kanryo Higaonna studied martial arts in Kien province (apparently southern Shaolin) in 1874 and, in 1905, opened a Dojo in the city of Naha. His art was called Naha-Te. Miyagi was his personal disciple or Uchideshi. Goju Ryu is the original Okinawan Karate.

—**Wado Ryu** was created in 1939 by Hironori Ohstuda. Ohstuda originally studied Shindo Yoshin Ryu Jiu-Jitsu, then became a student of Funakoshi's but disregarded the heavy emphasis on hard technique and put more attention on cultivating the open tranquil mind necessary for blending with an opponent.

—**Kyokushin Kai** was created in 1955 by Masutatu Oyama. This is the most popular style in Japan and is a variant of the more circular Goju Ryu. Mas Oyama's style is known for their impressive breaking techniques but more practically for their Kumite, or free sparring, which is hard contact with little, if any, protective gear. The overcoming of fear is a central aim.

ACTUALLY, I WAS BORN IN KOREA. BUT I CHANGED MY KOREAN NAME.

CHOJUN MIYAGI   KANRYO HIGASHIONNA   HIRONORI OHTSUKA   MASUTATSU OYAMA

GOJU-RYU KATAS

KRACK!

Oyama made his reputation by killing cattle, bulls in fact. He would either kill them by chopping off a horn or punching them out—then chopping off the horn! Clearly, these were not bred as killing Spanish bulls but, nevertheless, impressive if not necessarily humane.

When I was studying Tae Kwon do, I had the opportunity to spar (supposedly no contact) with two Shoto-Kan Black belts from Japan. Even though their style was very linear and easy to dodge, their attitude and will to win was not.

In Karate—Okinawan, Japanese, or Korean—the opponent's incoming blow, whether a kick or a punch, is often (if it works) met with a parry or a hard block which is a strike. The blending and evading of, say, T'ai Chi Ch'uan is rarely if ever practiced and is not apparent in the kata or kumite I have seen, although blending and evading are rare in many T'ai Chi practitioners.

Blocking horizontally with the inside or outside of the forearm, high block with the elbow down, fist higher or a lower block, almost a straight arm fist aimed down; rising blocks with the forearm horizontal, and blocks with the shins when the incoming is low enough are typically how the opponent is responded to.

Block punch, kick punch block, block kick, block punch is usually how a kata goes, the intensity and agility required going up along with the rank. Ideally.

The bobbing, weaving, and slipping of Western boxing are absent ... which is why most non-traditional or contact Karate practitioners study some boxing.

Jiu jitsu, another fighting rather than sport-oriented martial art, is a category under which all the empty handed arts were grouped during feudal Japan. It was the art the samurai used in their arsenal, which was mainly, of course, the sword. Although Japan's original art, it was not until the late 16th century that it became a systematized art. A practical application of any art which is studied in

Jiu-jitsu is the notion of flow or the ability to move from one technique to another as needed. There is little atemi (striking) in classical bugei, since on the battlefield or off there were weapons (and often armor) involved. The grappling and joint locks and throws of Jiu-jitsu work whether or not there is armor. Unlike Judo, Jumite, or Randori, punches and kicks are clearly available and used when appropriate.

All Jiu jitsu technique involves using the opponent's strength against himself. Some styles more than others. "Ju" means gentleness or giving way, "Jutsu" means art or practice. This notion is the single most characteristic of the art and its offshoots, Judo and Aikido.

Aiki Jutsu,
Aiki refers to harmony with the universe and again Jutsu is the technique or art. Like Ch'uan in the Chinese arts, Jutsu is the creation of a discipline of study and practice.

SAMURAI ARMOR! FAR TO ACTUALLY WEAR STUDENT WHO GOES AS UESHIBA IS THE ONLY

There are several modern styles of Jiu-jitsu, one of the most interesting and popular is **Hakko-Ryu Jiu-jitsu created in the 1940s by Rynho Okuyama**. It utilizes the vulnerable acupuncture points of the body to create disabling but not permanently damaging pain, both by applying pressure through various locks and holds, and by hitting.

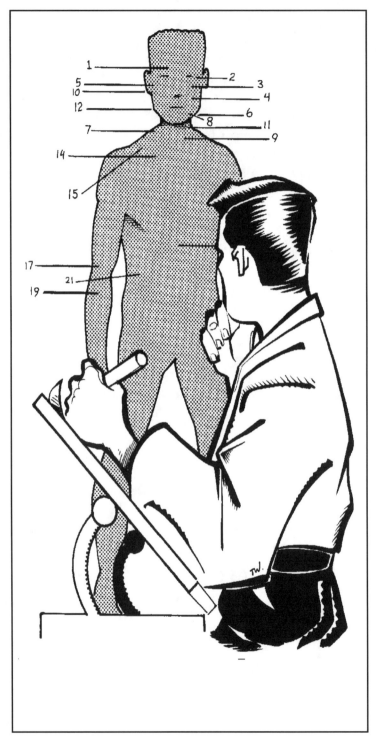

MANRIKI GUSARI OWES ITS ORIGIN TO **MASAKI TOSHIMITSU**, A SWORDSMAN. WEIGHTED AT EACH END OF A TWO FOOT CHAIN, IT CAN BE OFFENSIVE AGAINST MANY ATTACKERS AT ONCE, DISARMING, STRIKING, BLOCKING OR...

KRIS THE DOUBLE EDGED MALAYSIAN DAGGER, VERY **DEADLY!**

SAI FOUND IN CHINA, INDIA, MALAYSIA, AND OKINAWA.

POSSIBLE PRE-SAI; **TJABANG** CURSOR TO

TERRY WILSON

TA SHOA DZ SIMILAR TO THE OKINAWAN NUNCHAKU, IT IS THE FORERUNNER TO THE THREE-SECTION STAFF OR **SAN CHIEH PANG.**

A VERY ANCIENT WEAPON **BO** (IN JAPANESE) IS ABOUT 5' LONG IN JAPAN, 6' OKINAWA **BOJUTSU, KOBUTSU** AND, **KOBU JUTSU** ARE 3 OF ITS CLASSIFICATIONS

NAGINATA JUTSU A MOST DIFFICULT AND ELEGENT FIGHTING SPORT IN JAPAN.

WAKIZASHI JAPANESE WARRIOR SHORT SWORD. ONE HALF OF THE DAISHO THE OTHER BEING THE LONGER **KATANA**, IT WAS USED ALSO IN SEPPUKU.

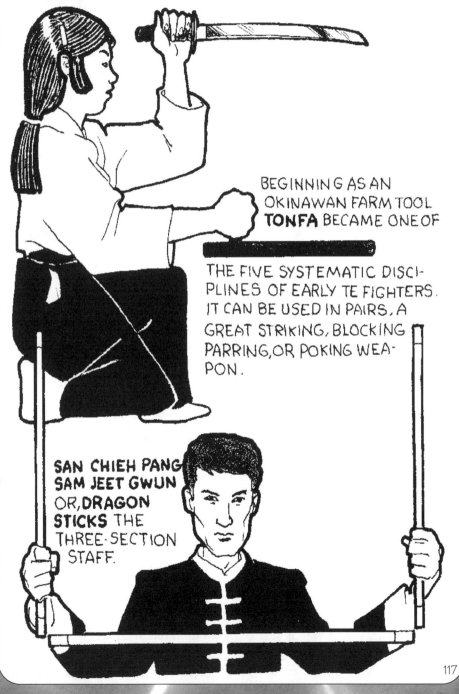

BEGINNING AS AN OKINAWAN FARM TOOL **TONFA** BECAME ONE OF

THE FIVE SYSTEMATIC DISCIPLINES OF EARLY TE FIGHTERS. IT CAN BE USED IN PAIRS, A GREAT STRIKING, BLOCKING PARRING, OR POKING WEAPON.

SAN CHIEH PANG SAM JEET GWUN OR, **DRAGON STICKS** THE THREE-SECTION STAFF.

JUDO

JUDO WAS CREATED BY JIGARO KANO IN 1882 AND IS BASICALLY JIU-JITSU WITH THE DANGEROUS STUFF TAKEN OUT -- AND WITH THROWING, SWEEPING, AND UNBALANCING TECHNIQUES EMPHASIZED.

This was done to turn Jiu-jitsu, which is more a fighting art with punches, kicks and Chin-na (grappling and joint locks) into a sport for the schools and colleges of japan. Kano believed the underlying principle of Ju was "to make the most efficient use of mental and physical energy." He felt that Jiu-jitsu, with its clear attacks and punches and kicking, didn't live up to his ideal, so he eliminated anything in the art he felt was not efficient.

Jigaro Kano was a friend of Gichin Funakoshi's and learned Atemi, which is hitting vulnerable spots on the body, from him. This is sometimes taught to black belts and above since it is pretty dangerous stuff and black belts in theory are more responsible. Kano also created an exercise regimen which is taught at the Kodo-Kan (the seat of Kano's Judo), called "Maximum Efficiency National Physical Education" (Seiroka Zen'yon Ko Kumin Taiku).

It is interesting to note that Moshe Feldenkrais, the founder of a form of bodywork based on bodily organization and efficiency, studied Judo

Judo, although a sport, is a formidable fighting art since its practitioners do actually compete and get the feedback required to develop the skill necessary to defeat another person—something lacking in most Karate and Kung Fu.

Wanting to develop a relatively safe sport, Kano also created a lot of rules concerning what is usable in a match and what is not. Obviously, for a game, clear rules are important, but here is the major difference between the sport and the martial art. The sport of Judo is an Olympic event and in Japan, like most things Japanese, is very formalized. The Kodokan in Tokyo, where Kodokan Judo (which is Kano's style) is practiced, houses thousands for its competitions.

AIKIDO

Aikido was created by Morihei Ueshiba and is the Japanese art that is closest in theory and application to the softest of Chinese arts, T'ai Chi Ch'uan. Aikido is a beautiful art to see when done by two people who are good at it. It has a flow that is wonderfully circular, with the attacker usually ending up being pinned to the ground or being "thrown" away (which the attacker deals with by rolling away).

Ueshiba started his martial arts training with Jiu-jitsu and Kenjutsu in 1902. Kenjutsu is the classical study of the Japanese sword. In 1912, he studied with the master of Daito-ryu, another sword school, Sokaku Takeda. He also studied Kodokan Judo with Kiyoichi Takugi.

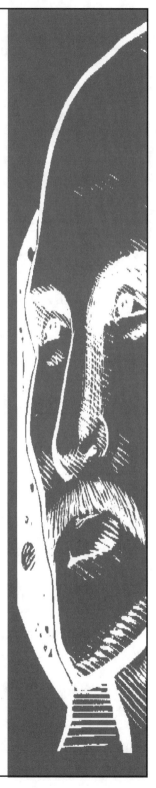

Ueshiba got involved with Onisuburo Deguchi, the creator of a religion called Omoto-Kyo.

DEGUCHI WAS FAMOUS FOR WHAT HE CALLED CHINKON KSHIN, OR "CALMING THE SPIRIT AND RETURNING TO THE DIVINE."

In 1924 Ueshiba went on an ill-fated trip to China in search of the Holy Land. (Some Pa Kua people I know think it was in China he was introduced to Pakua and was influenced by it. I don't know.) Anyway, in 1922 his disenchantment with his approach to the martial arts led him to break away from the traditional and create his own art which he called aiki-bujutsu although it was often referred to a Ueshiba-ryu.

In the Spring of 1925, he had received a fateful challenge from a naval officer who was a master of Kendo (Japanese sword). This was a sword fight and Ueshiba, being able to read his opponent's intentions, anticipated his action before it happened, and easily defeated him. Shortly after the fight he had a powerful enlightenment experience where he felt himself bathed in golden light, reborn, at one with the Universe. Thereafter he referred to his art as Aikibudo, signifying the way to harmony with the universe rather than Bujutsu, which is a warrior's art. After W.W.II the name was changed to Aiki-do.

Aikido techniques are practiced by two people—one the Uke, the attacker; the other Nage, the receiver, the one doing the technique. The practice is highly choreographed through the Kyu (below black belt) ranks and thereafter can be more open and freestyle (called Randori, the same as Judo freeplay).

SOME SCHOOLS DO RANDORI MORE AND EARLIER THAN THE ACQUIRING OF A BLACK BELT; IT DEPENDS ON THE TEACHER.

SHIHO-NAGE

1. Let's get into Shiho-nage with Ito and Tim to be presented here. Now Tim is about to throw a big right hand to Ito's jaw!

2. Ito blocks the throw, steps inside, and grabs Tim's hand.

3. Ito pivots and spins Tim around...

4. ... in preparation for ...

A FOUR SIDED THROW

5. ... the completion of Shiho-nage the four-sided throw which does not need a Hercules to perform, nor years and years of practice. Boy, is it effective! And in today's world effective, but quickly learned techniques, may be more practical for the streets and maybe the office. It is a break with the Tokyo HQ, not waiting years to develop, but this is the U.S. and we're always in a hurry.

Being as stylized as it is (and the pooh-poohing of competition in Ueshiba's style of Aikido), it is not taught as a fighting art, the techniques often being to large and time consuming to be effective. Yet, like all martial arts, it is the martial artist that is the art and Aikido techniques adapted to fighting are devastating.

AIKIDOS CLASS *of*

19 96

So the Uke attacks with a technique, the Nage blends with it and, with a circular leading technique, brings the attack to a conclusion with a lock or throw of some sort ... and the Uke, to prevent injury, rolls (Ukemi), flips, or falls, blending with the Nage's technique. If the Uke does not move with the Nage or resists Nage's technique, something breaks or dislocates.

There are several styles of Aikido. **Yoshinkai,** which is a harder Aikido style, emphasizes more strength and less Ki. The **Tomiki** style is one of the most interesting since its founder received his instruction from Ueshiba when Ueshiba was relatively young, and young is when the fire burns brightest. In Tomiki style the Aikidoists also compete with each other.

Kenji Tomki studied Judo under Jigaro Kano and then studied with Ueshiba in the 1920s. He received his 8th Dan black belt from the founder of Aikido which is very high—I don't think the founder gave anyone a higher rank. Anyway, he created his own system based on 17 basic techniques called K i h o n o - k a t a . Competition is held regularly.

> ## THE TRAINING OF KI IS WHAT ALL THE STYLES OF AIKIDO, AND IN FACT ALL THE JAPANESE ARTS, HAVE IN COMMON.

Ki is the Japanese word for energy, like the Chinese Chi. How it is trained depends on the school (it is usually done through some sort of breathwork) and how it is used in combat also depends on the school. Yet in Aikido, the use and cultivation of Ki play a more important part earlier in the training of the art than other Japanese arts. (This is a general statement, and again, depends on the teacher.) When Jigaro Kano witnessed Ueshiba's art, he considered it to be the highest budo (way of a warrior). Of course there are those who studied with the founder and teach their interpretations of the founder's art.

A black belt akido man has on his hakama (divided shirt). The wood genin ninja has on his outfit. Which is the more practical for on the ground grappling in a fight? In either case, roots of both styles have a Chinese influence, at least, where parts of Japanese cult comes from.

1.

Even during the old times a samurai could be formidable in unarmed combat.

2.

3.

4.

AAAA!

I'm **sorry**, but that piece of **Aikido instruction** won't fit into our **Dojo's** puzzle.

It is after all Ueshiba's art, and yet, like all martial arts, the particular emphasis and style is in the teacher's hands; so even though the tech-niques of Aikido are standardized and documented, there often are differences from Dojo to Dojo.

PHILIPIPNES

The root art of the Philippines is **Kali**. It is also called **Arnis** or **Escrima**, depending where on the island it comes from. Whatever the art was called, it helped the Filipinos defend their island from the invading Spanish, often

using knives and sticks against Spanish steel and armor. In fact the Filipino arts have been greatly influenced by Spanish sword play and most of the techniques have Spanish names.

In the 16th century, when Magellan arrived and tried to conquer the natives, he was defeated and his seasoned troops were sent limping back to Spain. Magellen himself was killed by the Chieftain Lapu Lapu; in the municipal museum in the province of Cebu is a picture of Lapu, a hero who killed a pirate.

It was when the Spanish returned with firearms that most of the Philippines were conquered— except for the fierce Muslim tribe called the Moros. Martial arts were outlawed, so, like the Okinawans under Japanese rule, the Moros preserved their martial arts in dance.

The Moros were never conquered by the Spanish. It wasn't until the Americans arrived in the early 1900s that they were dominated if not defeated. The Moro's were responsible for the development of the Automatic Colt .45 pistol. Apparently, in their religious fervor, a .38 would not do the job.

In W.W.II, Filipino martial artists were a gift to the United States in that they were excellent fighters against the Japanese, often using machetes or bolos to do the work. After W.W.II, many of the escrimador left the Philippines for the US to become farm laborers in California; many of them continued to practice their arts, often in secret. Indeed, many of the masters are still alive and teaching. Unlike most martial arts that are stylized and geared more for exercise and some formal sparring, Filipino martial arts are fighting arts which have been used in combat. With the coming of firearms, most martial arts systems have drifted away from the practicality and simplicity that combat requires. The masters of Chinese or Japanese arts often have not been tested through repeated encounters with death. It is generations in the past that their arts were thus challenged. Not so Escrima.

The arts of Kali, Escrima, and Arnis are considered to be bladed arts, and depending on the style, the weapon (often a stick in training) is from 18 to 30 inches long. It is also an open-handed art, but unlike Chinese or Japanese arts, weapons are taught first. The idea being weapons move faster, the end of a stick for example is much faster than the hand, thus building the speed and reflexes so that when the weapon is put down the speed developed remains.

The most popular of styles in the U.S. is Serrada, which was the personal style of the late Angel Cabales. It is a tight inside style which utilizes a short stick (18-20 inches) and a stand-your-ground attitude. Like other styles, the limbs are a favored target. The art is primarily trained through the practice of various drills defending against the 12 angles of attack in Serrada. It is pretty much the Wing Chun of Escrima, with its emphasis on small swings of the stick, not going past the swinger's shoulders at the end of the stick's travel. The umbrella block is where its compactness really shows compared to the large swinging style of Largo Mano.

Largo Mano, on the other hand, is very mobile with a longer stick, the strike often thrown while on the move, usually on the far side of the opponent's weapon. Largo Mano is done at "weapon's range" which is outside the range of the opponent's punch or kick, while the opponent is within range to be hit by the escrimador's weapon. Body positioning is important; the facing of the shoulders can mean being in or out of range. Like Serrada and Doce Parres styles, the

closest weapon goes for the closest target. In Serrada multiple hits are used at close range; windows of opportunity for a hit and speed are huge factors. Largo Mano style emphasizes mobility and one or two (more if needed) powerful hits. Two sticks can also be used in what is called crusada (or crossing), which is both a block and a strike and is classic Spanish technique.

In the 1930s, twelve masters of Escrima got together to systemize the art and the style known as Doce Pares is the result. They use a longer stick

than Serrada style, yet is closer to Serrada in range than Largo Mano.

There is work with two sticks or a weapon in each hand and one stick where the weaponless hand is used for trapping and checking or covering the opponent's attacking hand while the weapon strikes. The weaponless hand is called the "live hand." In the style of Ben Largosa, who studied with Floro Vilabrille (who studied with Felicissimo

Dizon, the creator of the DeCuerdos system), the hand of the opponent that holds the weapon is the target. Defanging the snake he calls it.

BRAZIL

Capoeira is an art developed by the descendants of African slaves brought to Brazil by the Portuguese. The exact origin is unknown, yet it is clearly a Brazilian art, and its like is seen nowhere else, even though there is dance in Africa that is in some ways similar.

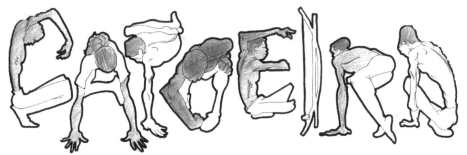

To attend a class is as much a journey into the culture of a country as a martial arts class. Unlike any other marital art I know of, the use of musical instruments is ever present and all Mestre (Masters) of the art would agree that it would not be Capoeira without them.

Capao is a Portuguese word which means rooster. It is also the name of a small partridge which, like a rooster, fights to maintain its territory. In fact, some earlier Capoeistra's dressed in feathered head-pieces for the Roda. The Roda is the game of Capoeistra, the people playing the instruments, the two "fighters," and the circle of Capoeistra each waiting their turn.

In the late 19th century, Capoeira had a rotten reputation as being the fighting style of the criminal and underclass (a rusty razor held between the toes was the favored weapon). Capoeira, perhaps the most acrobatic and contortionist of martial arts, the Capoeistra often delivers kicks while in a handstand or cartwheeling past their opponent. Since it had such a nasty reputation, it was discouraged and outlawed. For their part, the Capoeistra often made trophies of police batons.

In 1930, a revolution put **Getulio Vargas** in charge. He stopped the repression of Capoeira and in 1932 Mestre Bimba opened a school to the public. **Mestre Bimba** also systematized Capoeira, which had become pretty sloppy because of its long repression. He called his style **Capoeira Regional** and he was very concerned with the fighting aspect of the art.

Another style, **Capoeira Angola**, is considered a more playful style popularized by a contemporary of Mestre Bimba, **Mestre Pastinha**. Some time in the late 19th century, the central musical instrument of Capoeira, **the Berimbau**, came into use.

It is a single string instrument, a bow with a steel string. A hollow gourd is attached to the stick of the bow near the bottom, but not touching the stick. A thick coin is held between the string and the wood of the bow and is moved for different notes. A thin stick held in the other hand is used to either hit or be moved across the string like a violin.

The player of the Berimbau commands the Roda. The tempo chosen by the player of the Berimbau determines the tempo of the two fighters. The "fight" is spontaneous but each fighter takes turns doing a technique and yet it can be done at breakneck (literally) speed, depending on the music of the Berimbau. It is mostly a kicking art, the hands more often being on the floor or as a counterbalance. Ache is the Capoeistra's word for Chi, and in fiery Roda there is plenty of it.

The Korean martial art of **Tae Kwon Do** is probably the most popular style of Asian martial art in the United States. If there is a karate school in Gump, Iowa, it will be a Tae Kwon Do school for sure.

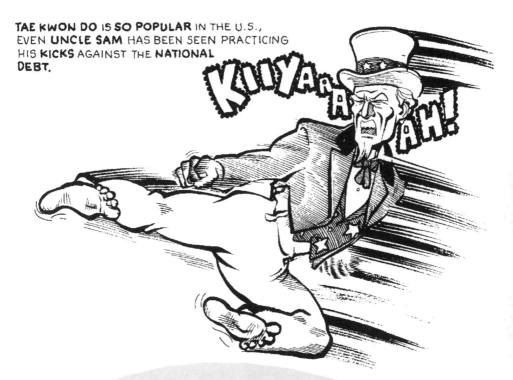

TAE KWON DO IS SO POPULAR IN THE U.S., EVEN **UNCLE SAM** HAS BEEN PRACTICING HIS **KICKS** AGAINST THE **NATIONAL DEBT.**

More Hwa Rang Do

The **Hwa Rang** were royalty who studied Confucian philosophy, archery, military tactics, and Tae Kwon Do—which later was called **Subak**, considered the native fighting art of Korea. Some sources say the Hwa Rang began in the **Silla Dynasty** (638-935), others say the **Koryo Dynasty** (935-1392). During the 1500s AD there was a decline in Subak's popularity because Korea was becoming more peaceful—no one was invading them—so scholarly pursuits rose in popularity. In 1909, the Japanese invaded Korea and, like any good invader, they immediately banned the practice of all martial arts. This naturally caused a great revival of martial arts in Korea.

139

It was also at this time that many Koreans fled to China, where many studied martial arts and returned later to spread the teaching and influence the native art. *(Some called the art at that time Tang Su or Tang Hand—sound familiar?)*

In 1943 Judo and Karate were introduced; of course there was a lot of interest, further influencing the maturing Korean martial arts.

The earlier Korean martial art of Tang Su (also called Kwon Pup Tae Kwon and Subak) was restructured after the defeat of the Japanese in 1945. A Korean military officer began teaching Tae Kwon to the newly formed Korean Armed Forces and in 1919 brought Tae Kwon Do to the U.S., demonstrating the art to U.S. troops at Fort Riley Kansas.

Modern Hwa Rang Do, "The Way of Flowering Manhood," has an extensive and far-reaching repertoire that includes acupuncture, the study of mind control (e.g., clairvoyance and ESP), as well as many fighting techniques.

THE YI DYNASTYS GOVERNMENT (1392-1910) ACTUALLY DISPANDED THE **HWARANG** FORCING IT TO GO SECRET IN THE MOUNTAINS AND BUDDHIST MONASTERIES. FROM THERE IT WAS HANDED DOWN FROM MASTER TO STUDENT UNTIL GRAND MASTER SUAHM DOSA PASSED **HWARANG DO** TO THE LEE BROTHERS, **JOO BANG LEE** AND **JOO SANG LEE**. SUAHM WAS THE 57TH GRAND MASTER; HIS SUCCESSOR IS **JOO BANG LEE** .THE 58TH.

THE FOUR MAJOR PATHS OF STUDY ARE 1.INTERNAL POWER: **NAE GONG,** 2.EXTERNAL POWER: **WAE GONG,** AND 3. WEAPON POWER: **MOO GI GONG,** 4.MENTAL POWER: **SHIN GONG!** **HWARANG DO** IS SO WIDE IN SCOPE ,THERE IS SOMETHING FOR **NEARLY EVERYONE**: HEALING ARTS, ESP, COMBAT...

AND YOU THOUGHT YOU HAD TO GO TO **KOREA,**TO FIND THE **HWARANG DO** WORLD HEAD~ QUARTERS, WELL IT'S IN **DOWNEY CALIFORNIA,U.S.A.**

In 1955, a collection of Tae Kwon and Subak masters decided to collectively call the arts **Tae Kwon Do** upon the suggestion of the now general **Choi Hon Hi**; in 1966, Hi created the International Tae Kwon Do Association. Tae Kwon Do (which means **"The Way of Kicking and Punching"**) has in its repertoire more kicks than either the Okinawan or Japanese arts.

FATHER OF AMERICAN TAE KWON DO, MR. RHEE'S STUDENTS INCLUDE CONGRESSMEN, SECRET SERVICE/TREASURY DEPT. PEOPLE, PENTAGON OFFICERS, TEXANS, AND **MANY** OF THE EARTH'S **TOP** EXPONENTS OF **TAE KWON DO**. A GOOD BUSINESSMAN, MR. RHEE'S PROMOTIONAL ACTIVITIES AND FILMWORK HAVE HELPED TO **PROTECT** AND **ELIVATE** TAE KWON DO AS AMERICA'S **MOST** POPULAR MARTIAL ART.

I WISH **MY** FRIEND BRUCE WAS HERE.

It is also one of the more popular arts, specifically in the full contact arena.

HERE HE IS, GEN. CHOI HONG HI. HE WAS THERE ON THE **APRIL 11, 1955** MEETING OF **KOREAN MARTIAL ARTS MASTERS** WHO ACCEPTED THE NAME **TAE KWON DO**, WHICH GEN. CHOI DEVELOPED AND SUBMITTED. A KOREAN PATRIOT, HE'D LEARNED CALLIGRAPHY AND **TAE KYON** FROM HAN IL DONG. HIS ACTIVITIES DURING THE **JAPANESE** OCCUPATION BEGAN GETTING HIM IN TROUBLE. KOREA AND MARTIAL ARTS **OWE MUCH** TO HIM.

Many professional fighters started with Tae Kwon Do because **Jhoon Rhee**, one of General Choi's students, was one of the first Karate men to promote the use of protective gear as well as full contact in America.

143

I studied Tae Kwon Do back in 1975 and, at the time, I was proud of the fact that my school did point contact, or no-contact where the punches and kicks were stopped. Basically the reason I was proud of it was simply because I belonged to that particular school. Well, **Jhoon Rhee** had a school right down the street and we were constantly bad-mouthing the place, considering it modern and non-traditional.

THE POSITION OF THE HANDS AT JHOON RHEE'S SCHOOL WAS CHANGED AND EVENTUALLY MORE WESTERN BOXING TECHNIQUE BEGAN TO APPEAR. HEAVEN FORBID.

When I was a purple belt (which was the belt below brown), two black belts in Shoto-kan arrived at the school from Japan and I had the opportunity to spar with them. Even though their art also was "no-contact," their intensity often overrode their caution. The study of willpower and strong intent was not a strong pursuit in my school where the cultivation of perfect technique was. Well, I found out which was more important in a fight.

HELLO GIRLS AND BOYS!
MY NAME IS **BONG SOO HAN;** I
STUDIED **HAPKIDO** IN KOREA UNDER
ITS FOUNDER **YONG SHUL CHOI**. I MET
FILMMAKER **TOM LAUGHLIN** IN
1971 WHILE GIVING A DEMON-
STRATION AND DOUBLED FOR HIM
IN **BILLY JACK**. CHOI HAD STUDIED
DAITO-RYU-AIKI-JUTSU FOR **40 YEARS**
IN JAPAN FROM **SHOTAKU TAKEDA**
BEFORE DEVELOPING **HAPKIDO** IN 1939-40.

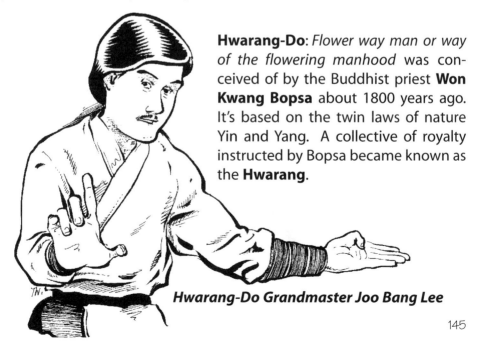

Hap Kido was founded in 1940 by Yeng Shui Choi. Choi studied Daito-ryu Aiki Jutsu (which was one of the arts Ueshiba the founder of Aikido studied) and combined it with Hwa Rang-do and Tae Kwon Do. Hap Kido is more fluid and circular than Tae Kwon Do, which is what one would expect with Aiki Jutsu as one of its foundational arts. Also, because of the Aiki Jutsu, it incorporates more locks, throws, and grappling than Tae Kwon Do. If you saw the movie *Billy Jack*, Hap Kido is the martial art that was used in the film.

Hwarang-Do: *Flower way man or way of the flowering manhood* was conceived of by the Buddhist priest **Won Kwang Bopsa** about 1800 years ago. It's based on the twin laws of nature Yin and Yang. A collective of royalty instructed by Bopsa became known as the **Hwarang**.

Hwarang-Do Grandmaster Joo Bang Lee

145

Tang Soo Do is a modern art, even though the name Tang Soo or "Chinese Hands" is what earlier Okinawan Karate was called. It was created by Hwan Kee who, after having mastered two esoteric Korean arts called Tae Kyun (not Tae Kwon) and Soo Bahk, traveled to Northern China. There he learned what he called the Tang method. I don't know what it was, since Tang is not a school of martial arts inside of China. It was some form of Shaolin, to be sure, and he combined all three of the arts into Tang Soo Do.

I t
is another no-contact art and
although one famous Tang Soo Do practitioner in
particular did incredibly well in point Karate competition,
he was soundly defeated when he entered the ring with gloves
on. This is not to say in a fight the traditional or modern is a better fighting art. My point is that within the context of the rules
of sport contact Karate, the people who have trained
themselves for years how not to hit people ...
lose.

The ranking system is similar to Karate, although the Kata are called Hyung and the Dojo (school in Japanese) is the Dojang. The arts are more simi-lar to Japanese Karate than to Chinese Kung Fu, although an art like Hap Kido is—or can be—more flowing and Hwa Rang Do can be softer than Tae Kwon Do.

Must be a **Hapkido** student practicing his **flowing** technique.

THAILAND

Muay Thai is the "fighting" art of Thailand. Also called **kickboxing**, it is an art that professionals often do with gloves, groin protector and anklets. The punches are similar to Western boxing and for good reason -- their punching techniques, as well as the slipping and dodging of punches, are imports from the West. Of course, Muay Thai was influenced by the Chinese arts, particularly during the Ming Dynasty.

The kicking, of which the **round kick** is the most frequently used (kicking with the shin, not the foot), is very powerful since the fighters, unlike most marital artists, really try to do damage to their opponent. The other preferred kick is a **pushing** sort of front kick. Elbows and knees are used and it is common to lock one's hands around the opponent's head and hammer away with knee blows to the abdomen and ribs. Professional full-contact Karate "fighters" have studied some Muay Thai, at least learning how to deliver a round kick with power.

Muay Thai fighters train like monsters -- after all, they are professionals and the style is bullying and tough. It's gaining popularity in the U.S., not as a spectator sport so much as a martial art you can go and learn. There are no Kata, only a few drills, and sparring; it's an art for people who want to learn how to fight.

Battling milkman using a **MUAY THAI** elbow strike...

...then a follow up!

NINJUTSU

The closest thing to a Ninja in 20th century America is a Green Beret or a Navy SEAL or some other professional specializing in the covert execution of missions requiring such skills as information gathering, wilderness survival, combat strategy and execution, and above all, stealth...

In 7th century Japan, there were people (called Yamabushi or mountain

ascetics) who, for various reasons, were fugitives from the government. Some were simply people who wanted the freedom to practice their own religion, some were criminals, and there were some who had survived battle and didn't commit seppeku (ritual suicide) for whatever reason but clearly they preferred life. (The samurai called them cowards. I am sure they thought the samurai naive.)

SINCE THEY WERE FUGITIVES, SECRECY AND STEALTH, ALONG WITH SURVIVAL AND COMBAT SKILLS, WERE PRETTY IMPORTANT. THESE WERE THE FORERUNNERS OF THE NINJA.

Prince Shotuku was the first to employ Ninja for his own use. Samurai families often had some in their employ. In fact the Shogun Lemitsu Ieyasu used several hundred Ninja to kill about 40,000 Japanese Christians hiding in a castle at Shimbaru (a strange irony, since the Ninja clans began as a people fleeing religious persecution). There were several important Ninja families, each of whom were very secretive and untrusting of outsiders.

CONTRARY TO LEGEND AND CINEMA ONE MAY NOT HAVE TO LOOK **ANY FURTHER** THAN ONE'S **DENTIST, BARBER,** OR **BUSINESS EXEC.** TO FIND NINJUTSU PRACTITIONERS OF TODAY FOR **HEALTH, HARMONY, SURVIVAL TRAINING,** AND MORE. NOT THE MURDEROUS SNEAKY KILLERS POPULARISED BY FICTION. IN THE **U.S.** HERE ARE THREE **TOP EXPONENTS OF NINJUTSU:**

BUD MALMSTROM

BONNIE MALMSTROM

STEPHEN HAYES

THE 3 NINJAS

The Ninja employed many ingenious weapons, strategies, and potions to achieve their ends, which was often information gathering, killing, or both. **They started training early in childhood for the rigors of the job.**

Although Ninjutsu has had a revival in this country the art has pragmatism as a central theme. The empty hands combat techniques reflect this as most of it is jiu jitsu. The cultivation of Ki, like in other Japanese arts, is important not only for fighting techniques, but the invisibility that Ninja are famous for require an awareness of their surroundings and an ability to "become" and blend with those surroundings, and that requires having a strong sense of energy.

INDONESIA

Pentjak-Siliat, sometimes called simply Pentjak -- or sometimes only Siliat -- is the primary fighting art of Indonesia.

According to *Asian Fighting Arts*, by Robert Smith and Donna Praeger, the origins of the art are found in China and, like many Chinese arts, were influenced by the observation of animals. The origin Story goes:

A peasant woman went to fetch some water; at the stream she wit-

nessed a fight between a tiger and a large bird. According to the story, both died (one helluva bird), and when the husband finally found his wife he tried to hit her for taking so long. Well, she dodged the blow, of course, using the "technique" she observed in the fight. Then the woman taught her husband, just as Wing Chun had taught her husband the art.

BANDO, INTERPRETED "WAY OF DISCIPLINE", "SYSTEMS OF DEFENCE" AND, "ART OF FIGHTING OR COMBAT." **MAUNG GYI** INTRODUCED **BANDO** TO THE U.S. ON **APRIL 3, 1960.**

KUNG TAO DOES NOT HAVE MANY VARIATIONS, BUT FROM VILLAGE TO VILLAGE OR CITY TO CITY, THE **FIGHTERS** WILL HAVE THEIR **OWN VARIATIONS.** RIVALRIES CAN BE **INTENSE!**

Bando is another art based on animal movements. It, like Muay Thai, utilizes kicks and punches, but then moves into locks and pins.

Kung Tao is a Chinese martial art in Southeast Asia. It is influenced by the "native arts" ... which were strongly influenced by Chinese arts.

The end.

153

About the Author and Illustrator

Ron Sieh has been involved with the martial arts since 1972, when he dabbled in boxing. Since then he has studied Tae Kwon Do, Tai Chi Ch'uan, Hsing I Ch'uan, and Escrima -- and dabbled in many more. He is the author of ***Tai Chi Ch'uan, Hsing I Ch'uan: the Internal Tradition***, described in *Prediction* magazine as "simply the best book I have ever read on any martial art."

Terry Wilson got off to a great start as a cartoonist and hasn't stopped since. By 1982, he had won best cartoonist in the Los Angeles Universities, first place in on-the-spot competition, and two first place awards in the Southern California Cartoonists conference while attending Cal State University of Northridge. Since then, Mr. Wilson has illustrated dozens of books, comic books, and branched out into designing everything from logos to sports clothing.

INDEX